D1079837

Included in the series:*

* Also published in French. Other titles to appear.

Planning education in and after emergencies

Margaret Sinclair

Paris 2002
UNESCO: International Institute for Educational Planning

The Swedish International Development Co-operation Agency (Sida)
has provided financial assistance for the publication of this booklet.

Published in 2002 by the United Nations
Educational, Scientific and Cultural Organization
7 place de Fontenoy, F 75352 Paris 07 SP
Printed in France by Pierre Finot
Cover design by STEDI

ISBN 92-803-1225-1

Fundamentals of educational planning

The booklets in this series are written primarily for two types of clientele: those engaged in educational planning and administration, in developing as well as developed countries; and others, less specialized, such as senior government officials and policy-makers who seek a more general understanding of educational planning and of how it is related to overall national development. They are intended to be of use either for private study or in formal training programmes.

Since this series was launched in 1967 practices and concepts of educational planning have undergone substantial change. Many of the assumptions which underlay earlier attempts to rationalize the process of educational development have been criticized or abandoned. Even if rigid mandatory centralized planning has now clearly proven to be inappropriate, this does not mean that all forms of planning have been dispensed with. On the contrary, the need for collecting data, evaluating the efficiency of existing programmes, undertaking a wide range of studies, exploring the future and fostering broad debate on these bases to guide educational policy and decision-making has become even more acute than before. One cannot make sensible policy choices without assessing the present situation, specifying the goals to be reached, marshalling the means to attain them and monitoring what has been accomplished. Hence planning is also a way to organize learning: by mapping, targeting, acting and correcting.

The scope of educational planning has been broadened. In addition to the formal system of education, it is now applied to all other important educational efforts in non-formal settings. Attention to the growth and expansion of education systems is being complemented and sometimes even replaced by a growing concern for the quality of the entire educational process and for the control of its results. Finally, planners and administrators have become more and more aware of the importance of implementation strategies and of the role of different regulatory mechanisms in this respect: the choice of financing methods, the examination and certification procedures or various other regulation

5

and incentive structures. The concern of planners is twofold: to reach a better understanding of the validity of education in its own empirically observed specific dimensions and to help in defining appropriate strategies for change.

The purpose of these booklets includes monitoring the evolution and change in educational policies and their effect upon educational planning requirements; highlighting current issues of educational planning and analyzing them in the context of their historical and societal setting; and disseminating methodologies of planning which can be applied in the context of both the developed and the developing countries.

For policy-making and planning, vicarious experience is a potent source of learning: the problems others face, the objectives they seek, the routes they try, the results they arrive at and the unintended results they produce are worth analysis.

In order to help the Institute identify the real up-to-date issues in educational planning and policy-making in different parts of the world, an Editorial Board has been appointed, composed of two general editors and associate editors from different regions, all professionals of high repute in their own field. At the first meeting of this new Editorial Board in January 1990, its members identified key topics to be covered in the coming issues under the following headings:

1. Education and development.
2. Equity considerations.
3. Quality of education.
4. Structure, administration and management of education.
5. Curriculum.
6. Cost and financing of education.
7. Planning techniques and approaches.
8. Information systems, monitoring and evaluation.

Each heading is covered by one or two associate editors.

The series has been carefully planned but no attempt has been made to avoid differences or even contradictions in the views expressed by the authors. The Institute itself does not wish to impose any official doctrine. Thus, while the views are the responsibility of the authors and may not always be shared by UNESCO or the IIEP, they warrant attention in the international forum of ideas. Indeed, one of the purposes of this series is to reflect a diversity of experience and opinions by giving different authors from a wide range of backgrounds and disciplines the opportunity of expressing their views on changing theories and practices in educational planning.

Educating populations that have been affected by crisis or natural disaster is vital in the rebuilding of the community. Unfortunately, the number of conflicts worldwide is on the rise, and more and more countries are in need of emergency education.

There are a number of crucial issues to be addressed in countries in emergencies, such as food shortages, illness, and lack of housing for populations who have suffered from the crisis, or who have been displaced to a safer location. In this booklet, Margaret Sinclair argues that providing access to education should figure as a priority for organizations who offer support to such populations, as one of their goals is that children will at some stage return to a situation of normality, where they will need to find work and set up a life for themselves, hopefully better than that which they had previously experienced. Also, the education that they receive can help banish prejudices and tensions that exist between communities, and possibly even prevent any such conflict in the future.

Organizations and educational planners will find this booklet helpful, as the author presents issues such as funding, inclusive education, safety in schools, trauma healing, daily activities to be included in the curriculum, distance learning, and many more elements relating to education, which can help mitigate the short- and long-term consequences of crisis.

The IIEP is extremely grateful to Margaret Sinclair, a distinguished and experienced expert at UNHCR and UNESCO, for writing such a clear and inspiring booklet.

Gudmund Hernes
Director, IIEP

Composition of the Editorial Board

Preface

Grabo Refugee Camp, Grabo, Côte d'Ivoire

"I am 17 years of age. From 1991-4 I fought for the rebels in Liberia. I experienced plenty wicked things. Carrying heavy weapons, burying dead friends who died in action and worst of all witnessing the executions of captured enemies. I were force to carry on the execution of enemies. These things still affect my mind. My parents are in Liberia and I don't know where. I am the fourth child of my parents' eight children. I am the only one who is trying to go to school regardless of the suffering. I'm always sleeping here and there, no permanent home. Yet I am trying to go to school. Some fighters who knew me in Liberia are always encouraging me to go back to Liberia and take up arms again. I am suffering but I don't want to fight."

Othello Walker

Conflict, instability and disaster affect the lives of millions of people each year. Consequences can be dramatic, and populations which have been struck by such traumas are deprived of families, homes and basic personal possessions, as well as security, social norms and a sense of community. Among the most important needs to attend to are naturally health and shelter, but education is just as essential to help children and youngsters to live a normal life, and to prepare them for adulthood in what will hopefully be a more peaceful environment.

Children exposed to violence and aggression from an early age need to be educated in basic societal values, to develop a sense of respect towards each other and other populations, and to banish prejudices in order to live in a mixed community, thus reducing existing tensions. Education can develop positive attitudes and reflexes, which are important to confront such situations as war or natural disaster. It is vital also to develop an education system or a curriculum that best

9

caters to the needs of crisis-stricken populations, and to ensure that no social groups are excluded or denied the right to education. Equity and human rights are major issues when planning education in countries experiencing situations of emergency and reconstruction.

Several factors can hinder children from attending schools, among which are the language of teaching, concerns over personal safety – notably for girls –, the characteristics and capacities of emergency teaching staff, and so on. As in most developing countries, but in a much more vivid and complex way in crisis and reconstruction settings, the need for funding is pressing. The support of organizations – governmental and non-governmental – and donors is often paramount, albeit more in certain countries than in others. Without their participation, countries or areas hosting displaced crisis-affected children would experience great difficulty in providing what is necessary, and the process – which should often be one of immediacy and urgency – would be greatly delayed. On the other hand, issues of donors' co-ordination have to be dealt with, which requires definite skills.

In view of the importance of the subject, the Editorial Board of the IIEP Fundamentals of Educational Planning series asked a well-qualified and experienced person, Margaret Sinclair, to draft a document, which would serve as both a state-of-the-art examination of the present situation of education in emergencies and reconstruction, and a guideline for planning education in emergency and reconstruction environments.

Each context has different requirements. Emergencies call for immediate action, while reconstruction is a long-term process. The time required for readjustment and reconstruction varies from one situation to another. Margaret Sinclair summarizes, in a very clear fashion, current thinking on the planning and management of education in such situations. Building on concrete experience in a number of countries, she addresses in a very practical manner the question of how to go about introducing, providing and managing education in emergencies. She outlines the process of moving from an emergency situation to re-establishing a functional education system, while examining the role of education in preventing or contributing to dealing with conflict situations. The booklet considers the content and processes of education that serve as forces for social justice, respect, acceptance of diversity, conflict resolution, and those aspects of education that can inadvertently contribute to prejudice, stereotyping, misunderstanding and conflict. She also convincingly argues the importance of adopting a developmental perspective from the very first stages of working in the area of education in emergencies.

UNESCO and IIEP are increasingly called upon to provide educational responses in emergency and reconstruction settings. This booklet provides the groundwork, upon which the programme of the UNESCO Headquarters Section for Support to Countries in Crisis and Reconstruction and the International Institute for Educational Planning (IIEP) will be built.

Having led a distinguished career in educational planning and management, culminating in influential appointments at UNHCR and UNESCO, where she has broken new ground in policy and practice, Margaret Sinclair is certainly the most appropriate person to write such a booklet. For this, the Board is extremely grateful to her.

Françoise Caillods
Co-General Editor

Acknowledgements

The community of actors in the field of emergency education has met regularly and communicated by e-mail since 1999, an arrangement recently formalized through the Interagency Network for Education in Emergencies (INEE). The ideas and experiences noted in this paper draw on this interaction, as well as on the comments of field staff, teachers and students. The author would like to thank in particular Mr Chris Talbot for his unfailing support, guidance and encouragement, and his determination to develop a sound academic foundation for education in emergencies, Mr Asghar Husain for his insights into the process of reconstruction, Ms Nancy Drost, founding Network Coordinator of INEE, for sharing her vision of the Network, Ms Pamela Baxter for a long professional partnership, and for sharing her insights into developing a systematic approach to education for peace, conflict resolution and life skills, and her husband for his patience and support.

Contents

Contents

List of acronyms

CARE	Concern for American Relief Everywhere
CEDAW	Convention on the Elimination of All Forms of Discrimination Against Women
CIDA	Canadian International Development Agency
COMAL	*Comunidades Mayas Alfabetizadas*
CRC	Convention on the Rights of the Child
DANIDA	Danish International Development Assistance
EFA	Education for All
EMIS	Educational Management Information System
GINIE	Global Information Networks In Education
HIV/AIDS	Human Immunodeficiency Virus/Acquired Immunodeficiency Syndrome
INEE	Inter-Agency Network for Education in Emergencies
IBE	International Bureau of Education
IDP	Internally Displaced Person
IFRC	International Federation of Red Cross and Red Crescent Societies
IIEP	International Institute for Educational Planning
IRC	International Rescue Committee
ISCA	International Save the Children Alliance
NGO	Non-governmental organization
PEER	Programme of Education for Emergencies and Reconstruction (UNESCO)
SOMOLU	Somali Open Learning Unit
SOLU	Sudan Open Learning Unit

TEP	Teacher Emergency Package
UN	United Nations
UNDP	United Nations Development Programme
UNESCO	United Nations Educational, Scientific and Cultural Organization
UNHCR	United Nations High Commissioner for Refugees
UNICEF	United Nations Children's Fund
UNOPS	UN Office for Project Services
UNRWA	United Nations Relief and Works Agency
USAID	United States Agency for International Development
WHO	World Health Organization

Prologue: From despair to hope

The victims of conflicts and emergencies are people who have been through heart breaking, sometimes appalling, suffering. Yet in camps and settlements, villages and towns all over the world, they very often look to education as their major, or even their only, hope for a decent future. Schooling is their greatest hope for a life that will transcend the poverty that breeds violence, which in turn intensifies poverty. Education allows these people to overcome despair. The testimonies below illustrate the meaning and value of education in the lives of refugees and others affected by conflict and disaster.

A double amputee

Twenty-eight-year-old Abdul Sankoh is the headmaster of the camp school and one of its most tragic victims. When rebels invaded and almost captured Freetown, Sierra Leone, in January, 1999, Abdul Sankoh…fled into the bush. He was seized several days later as he foraged for mangoes and although he offered to act as a porter carrying food he was recognized by one gunman and denounced as a teacher and traitor.

The guerrillas burned down his village and Sankoh's accuser seized an axe from the victim's own home, forced him to the ground and slashed off his right hand. The rebel then amputated his left hand before cutting him around the mouth and slicing off part of his ear as he lay unconscious. "Go to the president (Kabbah)" the rebels taunted, as they did to many other war victims. "He will give you your arms back."

As he tried to make his way to safety, the heavily bleeding Sankoh was shot at and almost killed by friendly troops. … He eventually walked into Freetown with his wife and two children and helped establish a school which gives hope to hundreds of youngsters at the amputee center.

Source: Wilkinson, (2000: 7).

An Afghan doctor's story

War broke out in Afghanistan when Dr Ahmadzai was only four. Forced to flee, the family embarked on a three-day journey through snow-covered mountains, during which many people died of exposure. They were relieved to be taken to a refugee camp near Peshawar, Pakistan. The children were able to study at the refugee school, initially a large tent and subsequently a mud brick building. In time, Ahmadzai qualified for admission into the Islamia College Peshawar, for which UNHCR provided him with a scholarship. He views his educational opportunities as a ray of light, enabling him to cope with the dark time as a refugee and move towards a positive future. As a result, he was able to enter the country's best medical college. Upon his graduation, Ahmadzai's parents were overjoyed.

UNHCR later provided him with an internship to serve his community in a project for malaria control amongst Afghan refugees. Seeing the high level of resistance to standard drugs, Dr. Ahmadzai decided to study preventive medicine and gained a place at the *Aga Khan University*. He faced financial difficulties but was assisted once again by UNHCR. He plans to use his expertise to help his country.

Source: Dr H. Ahmadzai, personal communication (2002).

Essay from a refugee school

When peace education was first introduced in our school in 1998 most of us believed that peace cannot be learned and that it is the responsibility of the government to maintain it. On the day that the headmaster introduced the new peace education teacher, many of us were impassive to this new development but we attended the classes all the same.

Since then we have learnt important values and attitudes. We learnt the elements that bring about peace, unity and understanding between people. These include similarities and differences, handling emotions, empathy and mediation. These elements have changed our attitudes towards each other.

Peer mediation has also played a vital role in reducing student conflicts in our school. In addition, because the peer mediator bears the responsibility of mediating between students, he gains skills in mediation that will be valuable in future.

The students in Central School now highly appreciate the important skills for peace that we have learnt. I would also urge that efforts to spread peace education in the community expand, because peace is the major key in rebuilding our country.

Abdifatah Miyir Ahmed
Central Primary School
Hagadera Refugee Camp
Dadaab, Kenya

Source: UNHCR (2002b: 9)

I.   What is 'emergency education'?

"We, the governments, organisations, agencies, groups and associations represented at the *World Education Forum* pledge ourselves to:

(i)   mobilize strong national and international political commitment for *Education for All*, develop national action plans and enhance significantly investment in basic education; ...

(v)   **meet the needs of education systems affected by conflict, natural calamities and instability** and conduct educational programmes in ways that promote mutual understanding, peace and tolerance, and that help to prevent violence and conflict."

Source: World Education Forum (2000a: 8).

The *World Education Forum*, held in Dakar in April 2000, adopted a *Framework for Action* requiring countries to work towards the objective of *Education for All,* including a pledge to *"meet the needs of education systems affected by conflict, natural calamities and instability"*. This recommendation followed a Strategy Session at the Forum on the subject of *"Education in situations of emergency and crisis"*.

The theme of 'education in emergencies' came to the fore in the 1990s in connection with the concept of 'complex humanitarian emergencies'. Publications describing education programmes in the crises of Bosnia, Rwanda, Somalia, Sudan and elsewhere, used titles such as "Rapid educational response in complex emergencies" (Aguilar and Retamal, 1998) and "Education as a humanitarian response" (Retamal and Aedo-Richmond, 1998). Such 'complex emergencies' can last for years or even decades. They can include displacement of people across the borders of their country, thus forcing them to become refugees, and/or displacement of people within their own country. They can include ongoing conflict and ongoing insecurity within

21

countries, sometimes with the collapse of central or provincial government, and hopefully conclude with situations of post-conflict rehabilitation and reconstruction, enabling the nation to get back on track for social and economic development. In this broad sense of complex humanitarian emergencies, all programmes for refugees and displaced or conflict-affected populations, as well as disaster victims, are considered to be *'emergency'* programmes.

This use of the word *'emergency'* is broader than its use in everyday speech and in some assistance agencies. The Office of the *United Nations High Commissioner for Refugees* (UNHCR), the UN Refugee Agency, for example, has 'emergency teams' that travel at short notice to crisis locations to set up new offices or assist existing ones. These 'emergency teams' are deployed only for of a period of a few weeks or months until new posts can be created in those locations to cope with, what others would call, a continuing emergency. The use of the term *'emergency'*, with its overtones of sudden crisis, can also lead to debates as to whether post-conflict rehabilitation and reconstruction, which can be very difficult in the early stages, should or should not be considered as 'education in emergencies'. This problem is overcome by the Dakar formula of meeting the needs of education systems *'affected by'* conflict, calamity and instability. By definition, special measures (*alias* 'emergency education') are needed while populations are still severely *'affected by'* conflict, disaster or instability. This includes the early phase of post-crisis reconstruction, when special measures are needed – often under conditions of difficult logistics and insecurity – to provide temporary shelter and educational materials to enable children to resume schooling quickly when their regional or national education system had been almost completely destroyed.

For UNESCO, an educational emergency is a crisis situation created by conflicts or disasters which have *destabilized, disorganized* or *destroyed* the education system, and which require an integrated process of crisis and post-crisis support (UNESCO, 1999). This matches the Dakar approach. UNICEF has used the term 'emergency' in an even broader sense to include natural disasters such as floods and earthquakes, and human-made crises such as civil strife and war, as well as 'silent emergencies' such as HIV/AIDS, extreme poverty and children living on the streets (Pigozzi, 1999). In this booklet, however, the 'silent emergencies' are not included, except in so far as they occur during situations arising from armed conflict or natural disasters.

Definition of 'Education for children affected by emergencies'

"Education that protects the well-being, fosters learning opportunities, and nurtures the overall development (social, emotional, cognitive, physical) of children affected by conflicts and disasters."

Source: Save the Children Alliance Education Group (2001).

In this booklet, we first examine the dimensions of the problem. An estimated 1 per cent of humanity has suffered displacement from their homes or other consequences of conflict and disasters in the 1990s (Sinclair, 2001). We move on to identify and describe the principles which characterize good practice in educational response to situations of crisis and reconstruction. We next examine what would be good practice for government response to particular crisis and post-crisis situations. This is rather new as a field of study. After considering some issues regarding the roles of non-governmental organizations (NGOs), UN agencies and donors, we conclude by considering how education can help prevent conflicts and disasters, and by looking at the future development of the field of education in emergencies.

II. Dimensions of the problem

The 1990s saw complex humanitarian emergencies that became household names and created the growing interest in 'emergency education'. By the year 2000, conflicts in Afghanistan, Bosnia-Herzegovina, Burundi, Iraq, Sierra Leone, Somalia, and the Sudan, had left large numbers of their populations (over 400,000) as *refugees* in other countries. Other countries that generated such a number of refugees in the 1990s were Rwanda and Kosovo. As many as 39 other countries generated over 10,000 refugees in any one year also during this period. In 2001, there were an estimated 15 million refugees in the world, including about 7 million in populations categorized as 'assisted by UNHCR' (UNHCR, 2002a), and 3.7 million Palestinian refugees, assisted by the *UN Relief and Works Agency* (UNRWA) for Palestine Refugees in the Near East.

Many refugees were from the developing countries of Africa (3.3 million) and Asia (5.8 million). In the year 2001, some 500,000 persons left home situations so dangerous that they were recognized as *prima facie* refugees (*i.e.* receiving countries granted them refugee status on a group basis). Meeting the educational needs of refugees has required resources from both the host countries and the international community. *Hosting refugees is one of the scenarios considered in this booklet.*

Most of the countries at the centre of complex humanitarian emergencies suffered massive *internal population displacements* also. Statistics regarding internal displacement are less readily available, however. This is partly because there has been less international access to, and assistance for, internally displaced populations. Many *internally displaced persons* (IDPs) live in camps or settlements similar to those for refugees, but others live in the homes of, or alongside, normal populations where they are less conspicuous and more difficult to quantify. Natural or human-made disasters likewise lead to internal displacement, either on a small scale or sometimes covering vast parts of a country, as in the 'millennium' floods in Mozambique in 2000. The world total of persons displaced as a result of conflict and human rights violations in 2001 amounted to an estimated minimum of 25 million (see www.idpproject.org). This includes over 13 million

IDPs in Africa, over four million in Asia and over three million in Eastern Europe. *Camps and settlements of IDPs thus represent another important scenario for consideration in this booklet.*

Conflict, insecurity and instability pose the greatest challenges to education. Educators often make gallant efforts to keep education alive during times of war or civil conflict. Classes are sometimes held in the open air, in homes and basements, or in damaged buildings of various kinds. Such conditions represent a third scenario for consideration here.

There is always hope at the beginning of a process of *reconstruction* following conflict or disaster. During recent years, many countries have faced or are facing the task of reconstruction. In the year 2000, there were 12 large return movements of refugees to their homeland, and a total of almost 800,000 returnees. There were probably similar numbers of internally displaced persons who returned to their places of origin. Populations that had stayed in place through conflict or disaster have likewise to work to rebuild their communities and countries. The scenario of reconstruction of education systems after conflict, or disaster, presents a major challenge to educational planners and managers.

Every *crisis is different*, and there are no sure formulae for successful response. The response must always be designed from the 'bottom up', using some form of participatory appraisal, in order to achieve the best results in the least possible time. However, it is possible to identify general principles that have been found to improve the quality of response in many emergency situations. Some of these principles are explored in the following chapters by examining ways in which they have been, or can be applied, in the following scenarios:

• education for refugees;
• education for internally displaced populations, including those displaced by natural disasters;
• education in situations of armed conflict, insecurity and instability;
• education for reconstruction, after conflict or disaster.

First, however, we deal with some frequently asked questions.

III. Some frequently asked questions

Some people doubt that education is necessary in emergencies, or that special measures are needed in such situations. Others even suggest that education programmes might be counterproductive. These doubts are addressed below.

Is education needed in situations of crisis and disaster?

Some donors have taken the view that it is sufficient to keep emergency-affected people from dying and to look after their physical health: they do not consider education as part of humanitarian response. This attitude is changing as it becomes clear that education can be part of the solution to such crises, and that the absence of education will be destabilizing locally and may be a threat to regional and global security. Restoration of access to education is, moreover, one of the highest priorities of emergency-affected populations themselves, as it provides hope for the future. Education can thus be seen as an investment in solutions to crises, as well as being the fourth pillar of humanitarian response (alongside nourishment, shelter and health services: Midttun, 2000).

Reasons for education in crisis and post-crisis situations include the following:

- education can help meet the psychosocial needs of crisis-affected populations;
- education provides a channel for conveying survival messages and developing skills for conflict resolution and peace-building;
- education is needed to prepare for reconstruction, and social and economic development;
- education can provide protection from harm;
- education is a human right, promoting personal development and preparedness for responsible citizenship.

Will education for refugee populations or IDPs prevent their speedy return home?

No! Experience shows that displaced communities naturally long to return home when they can do so in safety and with dignity. Families who have recently been displaced will not delay their return home because of short-term emergency education arrangements. They will return home to reclaim their land or properties, or return alongside others for whom this is possible.

Most refugees want to repatriate

In April 1992, the Marxist Government of Afghanistan was defeated. Immediately large numbers of Afghan refugees who had lived in Pakistan for a decade began to return, despite the existence of good school and health facilities in the refugee camps. About one million refugees returned home in four months until fighting resumed in Afghanistan. Most were returning to rural areas with limited facilities, partly from homesickness and partly to reclaim their individual and community land and properties. A similar mass return took place in 2002 after the ouster of the Taliban.

It is true that special transitional measures may be needed, where refugees have spent many years as students in primary and secondary schools in refugee settlements and would have difficulties completing their education if they repatriated. However, the right to education cannot be denied over such a long period. Examples of this kind cannot be used to justify withholding education in early emergency.

Is there something special about education in emergencies?

Yes! By definition the people's lives and their education system have been disrupted. The population has special needs if it is to recover from the crisis and build a better future. One way of describing the special features of emergency education is in terms of *principles* that are important in many, or all, education programmes, but have been found by practitioners to be *especially important in times of crisis*. The principles can be grouped in various ways. In this booklet, we group them under *access, resources, activities and curriculum,* and *co-ordination and capacity-building.*

These principles can be presented in the form of standards that must be met or that can be measured as 'indicators' of the success of a programme. When considered as standards or indicators, the verbs used are different. The 'principle' might be *"Education should be inclusive"*, while the 'standard' or 'indicator' would be whether inclusiveness can be observed in the ongoing programme, as in *"Education is inclusive"*, or *"Is education inclusive?"*

Principles of emergency education

Access

- The right of access to education, recreation and related activities must be ensured, even in crisis situations.
- Rapid access to education, recreation and related activities should be followed by steady improvement in quality and coverage, including access to all levels of education and recognition of studies.
- Education programmes should be gender-sensitive, accessible to and inclusive of all groups.
- Education should serve as a tool for child protection and prevention of harm.

Resources

- Education programmes should use a community-based participatory approach, with emphasis on capacity-building.
- Education programmes should include a major component of training for teachers and youth/adult educators, and provide incentives to avoid teacher turnover.
- Crisis and recovery programmes should develop and document locally appropriate targets for resourcing standards, adequate to meet their educational and psychosocial objectives.

Activities/curriculum

- All crisis-affected children and young people should have access to education, recreation and related activities, helping meet their psychosocial needs in the short- and longer-term.
- Curriculum policy should support the long-term development of individual students and of the society and, for refugee populations, should be supportive of a durable solution, normally repatriation.

- Education programmes should be enriched to include life skills for education for health, safety, and environmental awareness.
- Education programmes should be enriched to include life skills for education for peace/conflict resolution, tolerance, human rights and citizenship.
- Vocational training programmes should be linked to opportunities for workplace practices of the skills being learned.

Co-ordination and capacity-building

- Governments and assistance agencies should promote co-ordination between all agencies and stakeholders.
- External assistance programmes should include capacity building to promote transparent, accountable and inclusive system management by local actors.

Source: These principles represent a personal synthesis of the views expressed in many practitioner meetings and reports, and the author's own experience.

Other principles could easily be enunciated, but those listed in the above box give an introduction to the concerns of emergency educators. As noted earlier, these principles are, in some respects, not very different from good practice in any education situation. So what is different about emergencies? What is the difference between education in emergencies and education in developing countries that face funding crises and other problems?

One difference is procedural. When the international humanitarian community takes responsibility for education, with funds given by various governments or other donors for this purpose, these funds must be spent responsibly and the needs of the beneficiaries must be met up to a reasonable standard of effectiveness. The principles presented here summarize the conditions found necessary for effectiveness.

A second difference concerns the needs of emergency-affected populations. Violent conflicts and disasters disrupt society, and the rebuilding of social and physical capital poses a major challenge. For this reason, such populations especially need good quality education. Moreover, the national and international communities suffer various costs as a result of conflict. It is particularly important that populations who have shown themselves to be at risk be provided with education that will build the foundations of future peace rather than a recurrence of conflict. Education alone cannot build and maintain peace, but has a major role to play in helping to stabilize it. For this reason, expenditures on curriculum renewal and enrichment with peace education are not to be considered luxuries for conflict-affected populations. Nor should environmental education and disaster-preparedness be considered luxuries in countries at risk of climatic and geological catastrophes.

A third difference of particular interest to educational planners is the short time scale and planning horizon imposed in emergencies. This imposition comes from both the urgency of the situation itself and the exigencies of international donors, who often work on an annual project cycle and thus find multi-year educational activities difficult to support in emergencies.

IV. Access to education and related activities in situations of crisis and recovery

Families affected by war and crisis give high priority to the restoration of schooling for their children. It is often their primary concern after they have access to food and water for nourishment, to some kind of shelter, and to health facilities. In this chapter we identify some key principles regarding access to *education, recreation* and other *'structured activities'*. The term 'structured activities' is used by child advocates to refer to any organized activities that bring children and young people together to engage in studies, games, artistic or cultural activities, community service and so on, notably in crisis and post-crisis situations.

The principle of access to education and related activities and Education for All:

the right of access to education, recreation and related activities must be ensured, even in crisis situations.

The right to education is spelled out in the *1948 Universal Declaration of Human Rights*, which states that *"Everyone has the right to education" (Article 26)*. The *Universal Declaration of Human Rights* has been widely adopted as an international standard as is made clear, for example, in the *1981 African Charter on Human and People's Rights*, adopted by the *Organization of African Unity*. The right to education is also included in numerous human rights conventions, including the *1960 UNESCO Convention against Discrimination in Education*, the *1966 International Covenant on Economic, Social and Cultural Rights*, and the *1979 Convention on the Elimination of All Forms of Discrimination Against Women*. More recently, the right to education has been re-asserted in the *1989 Convention on the Rights of the Child* which, at the time of writing, has been ratified by all countries except the United States of America (which largely respects its provisions) and Somalia (lacking a central government to ratify the Convention). The Convention

33

requires that countries in the international community assist each other in ensuring children's rights.

The right to education spelled out under these agreements is of greater, not lesser importance in emergencies, as it gives a lifeline of hope. The *Convention on the Rights of the Child* covers persons up to the age of 18, but does not, of course, suggest that the right to education be denied from that age on, and other human rights documents do not have this limitation. In fact, many crisis-affected young people in their twenties attend primary or secondary school, because their education was delayed, or disrupted by war or instability in their country, or because this is the only constructive activity open to them in refugee or IDP camps, or simply because higher education, which is included in the Convention, essentially caters to young adults.

All the above-mentioned human rights instruments stress the right to universal and compulsory primary education – and that it be free in the areas where it is offered – and that the ladder of educational opportunity should be open at secondary and tertiary level.

Access to education in the Convention on the Rights of the Child

1. "States Parties recognize the right of the child to education, and with a view to achieving this right progressively and on the basis of equal opportunity, they shall, in particular:
    (a)   Make primary education compulsory and available free to all.
    (b)   Encourage the development of different forms of secondary education, including general and vocational education, make them available and accessible to every child, and take appropriate measures such as the introduction of free education and offering financial assistance in case of need.
    (c)   Make higher education accessible to all on the basis of capacity by every appropriate means…

3. States Parties shall promote and encourage international co-operation in matters relating to education, in particular with a view to contributing to the elimination of ignorance and illiteracy throughout the world…"

Source: Article 28.

In some countries, even primary education is not free-of-charge due to a weak tax-base. In such situations, efforts are often made to help the most needy, such as exempting them from fees and providing them with basic materials. In crisis situations, where a high proportion of the population may be without significant resources, the international community should be encouraged to support free access to schooling. Such support is often given to refugee education (although the level of funding is often insufficient), but it may be lacking in other crisis-affected areas.

In addition to their commitments under human rights agreements, the world's governments have agreed on the objective of *Education for All*, both at Jomtien in 1990 and at Dakar in 2000. *Education for All* implies support for early childhood development and appropriate educational opportunities for children, adolescents and adults, including access to secondary and higher education. Internationally agreed targets have been set to attain *universal primary education* by 2015, and gender parity in school enrolments by 2005.

It is important to note that there is no clear distinction internationally between 'primary' and 'secondary' education. Primary education can represent the first five to eight, or even nine years of formal schooling. The distinction is one of administrative convenience and varies from country to country.

Refugee situations

The 1951 Convention relating to the *Status of Refugees* includes an *Article 22* dealing specifically with the education of refugees. This convention was developed in the context of refugees from the 1939/1945 war and subsequent political changes in Eastern Europe, and specifies that refugees must be admitted to the compulsory stage of education alongside nationals. It requires that states admit refugees to post-compulsory education on conditions no less favourable than those applicable to aliens generally. The Protocols agreed in 1967 extend the coverage of the 1951 Convention worldwide.

The *Convention on the Rights of the Child* specifies that governments may not deny access to education to any child or adolescent on their territory, no matter to what social group they belong. Thus governments may not deny young refugees or asylum-seekers access to education. There have been instances in the 1990s when governments have vetoed the education of refugee populations (e.g. Rwandan refugees in Eastern Zaire, 1994-1996) or the establishment of refugee secondary schools, and other instances where individual refugees or asylum-seekers were denied the right to education. This is contrary to the *Universal Declaration of Human Rights* and subsequent human rights instruments.

In fact, governments should ensure their compliance with human rights obligations by verifying that their school and college admission policies do not inadvertently prevent the enrolment of individual refugees, for example by insisting they provide documents such as birth certificates, identity cards, or records of previous schooling that refugees may not have at their disposal (having fled their towns or villages in haste, and perhaps having been robbed as they crossed the border by bandits). UN agencies and NGOs should draw the attention of governments to such situations. It is also preferable, for humanitarian reasons, to ensure that refugee students are not required to pay higher fees than local students do (even if higher fees are charged to aliens).

Access to higher education

After a visit from the *United Nations High Commissioner for Refugees* in 1997, *Makerere University* in Uganda issued a statement that refugees would not be charged higher university fees than nationals.

It seems reasonable to consider that the right to education includes the right for studies to be officially recognized. In the case of refugees, this should, in principle, mean recognition of their previous studies by the government of the country of asylum if they are seeking admission to national educational institutions; and the recognition of studies in refugee schools by the governments of the countries of asylum and origin. (See discussions below.)

Internally displaced populations

Governments are obliged by human rights conventions to provide full access to education to those of their population who are internally displaced. This can be controversial and difficult when there is internal conflict, but, at the very least, governments may not prevent communities from organizing schools or voluntary organizations from assisting them. Sometimes governments discriminate unintentionally, as in the case of a country in the Caucasus where internally displaced students did not receive textbooks because the books were still nominally allocated to the districts which the students had vacated. In the case of major natural disasters, governments may face resource constraints in providing schools for the internally displaced. It is important that resources for education are given high priority in appeals for external assistance to internally displaced populations.

Graça Machel, in her review of progress since her 1996 landmark report (Machel, 1996) on the impact of armed conflict on children, notes once more that many adolescents in conflict-affected countries have not mastered basic literacy and numeracy, and that they need accelerated learning programmes to help them catch up with the class level of their age group. She cites a remedial learning programme in Georgia which prepares displaced adolescents to re-enter classes at grade levels five, seven or nine (Machel, 2001).

Access to education for internally displaced children

"Internally displaced children face different obstacles than their refugee counterparts. Continued fighting and frequent dislocation complicates their access to education. In Azerbaijan, about one million Azeris were displaced outside the town of Terter. The same abandoned railway cars used to house 4,000 internally displaced people also serve as classrooms. Despite a shortage of books and supplies, teachers and students show up each day in railway cars that lack heat and glass in their windows. In the capital city of Baku, where displaced families occupy abandoned hospitals and other public buildings, schools for displaced children function without electricity and blackboards. Some classes are held in buildings with walls that have collapsed".

"Where government schools are available, internally displaced children may be prohibited from attending because they lack the identification documents

---

37

needed to enrol. In Colombia, families driven off their land by paramilitary or guerrilla groups have been forced to keep their identities hidden for fear of being targeted. As a result, their children have no access to health care or state services, including school. In 1997, the Sri Lankan Ministry of Education allowed children without birth certificates to attend school, but refused to allow them to sit for examinations or participate in sports."

Source: Machel (2001).

Conflict, insecurity and instability

Governments, by definition, have difficulty in ensuring the right to education in areas experiencing armed conflict, insecurity and instability. Education can sometimes continue if educators are adequately trained and committed. Classes were held in basements in Sarajevo during the early 1990s. The *Save the Children Federation/USA* trained communities in Bosnia to establish pre-schools during this conflict (Burde, 1999; Nuttall, 1999).

Major international efforts to support schooling in this type of situation include the distribution of educational materials and the development of open-learning approaches to teacher education in Somalia; and support for temporary schools in Angola using a version of the 'Teacher Emergency Package' approach described below. An outstanding example is *Operation Lifeline Sudan*, led by UNICEF in co-operation with NGOs, which has provided cross-border support for schooling in war-torn Southern Sudan, including education materials and some teacher training.

Reconstruction

In situations of local or national reconstruction, there is normally an effort to restore access to education, often in situations of resource constraint, which can include a lack of personnel and equipment to plan and co-ordinate the process. Other limitations on access may include discrimination against particular groups or regions. There were disputes in Rwandan villages in 1997 concerning the grades (years of schooling) to which Rwandan children who had attended refugee schools in Tanzania should be admitted, for example.

Assistance programmes should not focus solely on the reconstruction of basic education (a term which includes primary and often lower secondary education). The 1966 *International Covenant on Economic, Social and Cultural Rights* specifies that *"the development of a system of schools at all levels shall be actively pursued"*, as is indeed necessary if there is to be economic, social and cultural development; and the *Convention on the Rights of the Child* requires access to all levels of education. This is important also if there is to be a return of members of the diaspora, for whom secondary and tertiary education of their children is important.

In conclusion, it is important for education ministries, in countries affected by crisis or hosting refugees, to be aware of their obligations under international law to ensure access to education and not to prevent UN and voluntary organizations from supporting such access when the ministries lack resources for it. UN agencies, NGOs and researchers should be alert for situations where educational access is denied, sometimes unintentionally, and bring this to the attention of the governments concerned. It is important equally for donor countries to be aware of their obligation under the *Convention on the Rights of the Child* to help achieve this objective, as well as their pledge at Dakar to provide such assistance.

The principle of rapid access to education and related activities, and subsequent improvement in quality:
rapid access to education, recreation and related activities should be followed by steady improvement in quality and coverage, including access to all levels of education and recognition of studies.

Structured activities for children and young people, such as education, recreation, expressive activities and community service, have been observed by humanitarian workers to support a healing process, lessening the incidence of trauma-related symptoms and enabling the youngsters' natural resilience (UNHCR, 1997a).

Education and related activities can also bring to light cases of severe post-traumatic stress, requiring specialized individual attention. This psychosocial dimension has major implications for the timeframe of response, since delay can have adverse effects. Experienced humanitarian workers have observed that the reinstatement of schooling also has a beneficial effect on the psychological condition of adults, and eases the burden on mothers who may be suffering from trauma, and may have difficulty finding food, water and firewood for feeding their families. Ideally, there should be rapid progress towards recreating a unified system of education and making arrangements to formally begin a new school year or complete an interrupted one. This is of great importance to families and young people.

Psychosocial needs of crisis-affected children and adolescents

Exposure to conflict or other traumatic events can lead to problems such as:

- withdrawal from social contact;
- not playing, laughing or expressing emotions;
- sadness and guilt;
- aggression;
- sleeping difficulties;
- nightmares and bedwetting;
- psychosomatic disorders;
- flashbacks;
- inability to concentrate in school.

Source: Macksoud (1993); Tefferi (1999).

Refugees and IDPs often initiate schooling themselves, even in the open air and without supplies or schoolbooks. It is important that humanitarian agencies provide immediate support such as materials and plastic sheeting for shelter. This may serve to prevent schooling in post-conflict displacements from becoming a mechanism for indoctrinating children with hatred and a desire for revenge. The international community did not support refugee schools in Zaire in 1994, and it is possible that some teachers who lacked blackboards and reading and writing materials for students may have engaged in such indoctrination. Humanitarian assistance to education carries with it the possibility and duty of insisting that schooling serves the interests of peace rather than war.

Practical aspects of rapid response include the deployment of teachers – often requiring training for volunteers, shelter arrangements, education supplies and materials. Education supplies may be locally procured or, if necessary, imported. There has been much discussion over the use of 'education kits', but there are many disadvantages to this approach (for a review of this debate, see Sinclair, 2001: 57-66). Education materials, such as textbooks, may be difficult to obtain for refugees absent from their own countries, or within a country where textbook production capacity has collapsed or distribution systems have failed.

The 1994 refugee education programme for Rwandan refugees in Ngara, Tanzania began a few weeks after the arrival of the refugees, at least in Lukole camp. The first stage in this programme was the setting up of simple educational and recreational activities which was followed by a second stage that involved the distribution of education materials (a '*Teacher Emergency Package*') and hiring and training teachers for all the camps. This major inter-agency operation led to the conception of a three-phase response to emergency. Phase One covered locally organized simple educational and recreational activities; Phase Two, the establishment of an education system in all localities; and Phase Three, the restoration of a curriculum, teacher training and examination (UNHCR, 1995; Aguilar and Retamal, 1998). Each emergency scenario is different, however, and there is now greater emphasis on immediate restoration of schooling. Moreover, there is an attempt, wherever possible, to formally start a new school year at the normal date as a psychological marker of normality. Hence the idea of three specific phases has faded somewhat.

Rapid response is an ideal that is not always achieved. Sometimes this is due to logistic difficulties, such as bad roads and limited airport capacity for freight. Sometimes host governments, UNHCR and donors hold back from providing rapid support for the schooling of displaced children so as not to raise hopes for an immediate spontaneous return. In general, however, the increased awareness of the psychosocial needs of children and adolescents and of rights under the *Convention on the Rights of the Child* have led to more

41

rapid response. In recent years, the Norwegian Government has supported secondments of emergency education co-ordinators through the *Norwegian Refugee Council* to assist UNHCR, UNICEF and UNESCO to act quickly. In one of the more effective examples, *Norwegian Refugee Council* educators reached Macedonia within a month of the arrival of Kosovo refugees late in March 1999, and, jointly with UNICEF, supported the refugee schools which had already begun in the camps in mid-April.

**Recommendations on education supplies
for rapid emergency response**

"How soon are supplies needed?

The aim is to create structured activities for children and adolescents in most locations within a month of displacement, and in all locations within three months. A unified education system should be in place for completion of the interrupted school year or for a new school year, not later than six months after the first major displacement.

"When should supplies be locally procured?

Where possible, it is preferable to procure education supplies in the country or immediate region concerned. In many cases this is feasible, especially where procurement is through organizations such as NGOs. Supplies obtained in this way may be cheaper (especially if transport costs are taken into account), logistics may be easier, and there will be a benefit to the local economy.

"When should supplies be procured internationally?

Where necessary, supplies can be sent from the UNICEF warehouse in Copenhagen or from UN or NGO regional centres, such as the UNESCO-*Programme of Education for Emergencies and Reconstruction (PEER)*, Nairobi. UNICEF often sends emergency supplies from Copenhagen, since procurement by local UNICEF offices requires various administrative approvals, which take time. UNICEF can send emergency education and recreation kits within a week, but with high airfreight costs, and the need for major logistic support for distribution on arrival. Sea freight takes several weeks but is less costly. Sending kits is appropriate when speedy local procurement by efficient NGOs is not practicable, and especially when procurement would otherwise be through a national government that lacks the capacity to work fast and cannot prevent diversion of resources."

Source: Recommendations of the *Inter-Agency Network for Education in Emergencies' Task Team on Learning Materials* (2001).

In displacement situations, it may take time to create fully functioning secondary schools due to the need to find teachers, textbooks and so on. It is important, however, to establish study skills classes for secondary school students as soon as possible, and to focus on the progression of students into full schooling. As well as providing encouragement for students to complete primary schooling, this also meets the aspirations of ex-secondary school students and the future needs of the society for educated persons.

The principle of inclusion:
education programmes should be gender-sensitive, accessible to and inclusive of all groups.

The phrase 'access to education' has a range of meanings, such as legal access, physical access, and access to education that is effective and appropriate. Perhaps a majority of the world's children who are out of school are denied access to education by poverty; and there are other barriers that prevent children from attending school, such as gender or disability. Emergencies may strengthen these barriers or create others.

Human rights instruments have set standards for inclusion. Since the 1948 *Universal Declaration of Human Rights* and the 1966 *International Covenant on Economic, Social and Cultural Rights*, there has been an emphasis on *educational access for the poor,* which includes free primary schooling and measures to promote access to secondary education. The UNESCO Convention against *Discrimination in Education* (1960) prohibits any discrimination in education on the grounds of race, sex, language, religion, opinion, national or social origin. The Convention on the *Elimination of All Forms of Discrimination Against Women* (1979) emphasizes gender equality in education.

In situations of emergency, it is especially important to involve ALL children and young people in organized activities, including education, to help them overcome the psychological consequences of the emergency and assist their reintegration into social networks. This means identifying ways in which *children from poor families* can be encouraged to enrol in, and succeed in, school. Community leaders, women's and youth groups can advise on policies and can help implement them. Children from poor families often have little encouragement in the home to succeed in education, and are often under pressure to sacrifice their schooling in order to support their families; by contributing to the family budget or by taking on various chores, however limited these contributions may be. *Child-to-child* tutoring may be required, as well as interventions such as systematic provision of second-hand clothes to the needy, free educational materials, and so on.

Situations of emergency can change the dynamics of *gender*, as regards school enrolment. One obvious reason for this is a lack of security, meaning that children – girls in particular – are not allowed to travel to school. A breakdown of social norms as well as insecurity may mean an especial reluctance to allow girls to attend school after puberty to avoid cases of sexual harassment or unwanted teenage pregnancies. Sometimes there are additional chores, such as queuing for food or water supplies, which keep children – again, girls especially – out of school. Sometimes, however, there is increased access to schooling due to proximity to schools within a refugee or IDP setting. There may also be increased access to school as a result of the provision of food and other basic requirements through humanitarian programmes, or even due to the lack of employment opportunities, (which lessens the 'income foregone' cost of schooling).

Special measures may be called for to meet the needs of older girls and teachers for decent clothing and sanitary materials. It is important to discuss gender issues with older students, parents, teachers and community groups, especially with girls, mothers, female teachers and women's groups.

Under emergency conditions, it is desirable to enrol girls in school at an early age so that they can make substantial progress in their schooling before puberty, and hopefully attain sustainable literacy and numeracy. This will also help them to continue with their schooling after puberty, if they so wish, since they will be better able to catch up on missed periods of schooling or to utilize distance methods of education if these are available. Communities may be encouraged to provide early childhood care and education for the under five-year-olds, so that girls can enrol in school at five years of age rather than being obliged to look after the youngest children in the family until a younger sister is ready to take over this role. In some locations, satellite lower primary schools with crèche and pre-school facilities might help increase the number of girls enrolling in schools.

Recommendations to prevent female drop out in *International Rescue Committee* refugee schools in Guinea

1. *To improve young girls' perceptions of their academic capabilities.*
   * Gender training programme for all teachers.
   * Showcase girls' work in early primary grades.
   * 'It's not too late' campaign for girls aged 13 or older to return to school.

2. *To increase adults' involvement in their daughters' education.*
   * 20-Minute a Day campaign for parents to hear their daughters read.
   * Parent/Daughter school days.
   * Female education campaigns in target areas of low enrolment or high drop-out.

3. *To provide academic support for girls who have no adult assistance.*
   * Assist female students living alone to organize study groups.
   * Organize an academic 'buddy system' where each of these girls is paired up with a girl from the next class up.
   * Organize monthly conferences with the Education Co-ordinator for the zone.

4. *To ease the economic burden that school poses for girls.*
   * Provide clothing.
   * Implement scholarship programmes for the very poor who are academically talented.
   * Provide a place in school for income-generating activities.

5. *To address reproductive health and contraceptive issues.*
   * Start contraception education sooner (at grade three).
   * Revise the contraceptive curriculum for upper primary, including negociation skills.

- Organize young men's social clubs to discuss responsible sexuality (girls' clubs already exist).
- Organize reproductive health seminars with parents.
- Experiment with conducting separate classes for pregnant students.
- Initiate co-operation with UN agencies and other international NGOs regarding sanctions for any worker who impregnates a student.

Source: Rhodes, Walker and Martor (1998: 21-23).

It is important for education and recreation programmes to ensure the fullest possible participation of *persons with disability*. This can include integrating children with moderate disabilities into normal schools and training the teachers on how best to help them. Other possibilities are to offer special classes for children and adults who are severely deaf or who have severe problems of vision, which may be practicable in a densely populated community such as a town, camp or settlement. Some individuals may be identified as likely to benefit from specialist educational institutions in the country concerned.

**Inclusive education in the refugee schools
for Bhutanese refugees in Nepal**

"There are 1,085 children with various disabilities in the camps, of whom about 30 per cent are hearing-impaired. These children are admitted into school at the same time as the normal children, although some flexibility in age is allowed. Only one type of disabled child is put in any one class and the children are normally seated in the front row for easy access to the teacher. Awareness programmes have been given to the community and all teachers. Each school has a special needs support teacher. The special needs support teachers receive training from the central office, after which they train the schoolteachers in how to deal with disabled children in their classes. The special needs support teacher also provides support and guidance to the disabled children. Where necessary, remedial classes are given to the disabled children after school hours. The special needs support teachers visit the homes to guide and train the parents so that they can assist their disabled children and monitor their progress. ...Contacts have been made with donors who have offered hearing aids or spectacles to the children after they have been tested physically."

Source: Brown (2001: 133).

Special groups found in crisis-affected populations may include *teenage mothers*, who became pregnant as a result of rape or the breakdown of social norms during war, *ex-child soldiers and adult ex-combatants* (McCallin and Jareg, 1996; see also the UNICEF reports on www.ginie.org), *working children* who have to support one-parent families or child-headed families, and so on. In some cases, it may be sufficient to encourage these groups to attend normal schools, while in others special measures may be needed. Adolescents and youth, whether working or ex-combatant, or deprived of access to schooling when they were younger, may benefit from condensed primary school classes that cover the essentials of five or six years of education in a period of three years, for example, and permit accelerated entry into the formal system.

Education of ex-child soldiers in Liberia

"In 1999, the accelerated learning project piloted in 20 schools (800 pupils) in four counties was scaled up to reach 6,000 pupils at schools in eight counties. The project condenses six primary school grades into three, and a child who goes through the programme can enter the regular 7th grade. Curriculum is compressed, focusing on skills development, and teaching methods are pupil centred. The success of the programme lies in the students' motivation, their readiness to learn because they are older, and support by their families and communities. A separate project seeks to facilitate war-affected youth's economic reintegration into their communities, by combining vocational training with literacy, numeracy and life skills training. Since activities began, 6,000 children have participated. Vocational training is now centred in agriculture and masonry – skills that are not only marketable but essential to rebuilding Liberia. Life skills, especially raising participants' HIV/AIDS awareness, has largely replaced the trauma counselling that was key during, and in the immediate aftermath, of war."

Source: Catherine Langevin-Falcon (2000) on www.ginie/org; for updated information, see www.ginie.org/ginie-crises-links/childsoldiers/liberia.html.

The principle of protection:
education should serve as a tool of child protection and prevention of harm.

Access to education is a human right that must be protected, since modern society uses educational institutions to help equip children and young people for modern life. Education is a tool, likewise, for protecting other rights of children and promoting their best interests. Education can and should help ensure the rights to life and health. Schools can disseminate life-saving messages to the community regarding particular health threats, sanitary arrangements, protection of the environment and so on – messages which can be passed to students, parents and participants in youth programmes. These messages should be reinforced and systematized over the longer term as part of education and youth programmes, and should then include education for conflict resolution, tolerance, human rights and citizenship.

Widespread access to education and other organized activities provides a means for identifying and helping children and young people in need of special help. Teachers and youth leaders can identify those who need help because of problems related to post-traumatic stress, sickness, malnutrition, disability, abuse and so on. Attendance at school, if in secure conditions, protects children from the risks of being recruited into other harmful activities, including forced labour, drug trafficking and prostitution. If the community is actively involved in identifying children who do not attend school, this can help identify children who are being exploited or abused in various ways.

**Schooling versus militia activities
in the *Democratic Republic of Congo* (DRC)**

"The connection between communities, teachers and education as a protective strategy for children is dramatized by this recent description from DRC:

Since war broke out in Congo in August 1998, civil servants and teachers have not been paid, so parents, who can afford to, pay the teachers. *'When the children do not bring any money, we forbid them to attend school'*, said the principal at the main primary school in the town. *'It's a difficult decision to make, but if we didn't, we would never receive any salary.'* As a result, thousands of children in the town don't go to school. Instead, they don crisp new (military) uniforms and march through the town's dusty streets singing rebel songs."

Source: Zajtman, cited by Sommers (2002: 12).

Education and youth work provide an opportunity to orient young people in conflict situations towards the importance of non-violent solutions to conflict and to explain their right, under *Article 38* of the *Convention on the Rights of the Child*, not to be recruited as child soldiers. *Save the Children Sweden* used this part of the Convention to discourage Sudanese adolescents in Kakuma refugee camp from joining militias as under-age soldiers.

Non-recruitment of minors

"States Parties shall take feasible measures to ensure that persons who have not attained the age of fifteen years do not take a direct part in hostilities [and] refrain from recruiting any person who has not attained the age of fifteen years into their armed forces."

Source: Convention on the Rights of the Child, Article 38.

It is important that schooling does not place children in potentially dangerous situations. School buildings may be the subjects to attack during conflict. Schools can also be targeted by militias for under-age recruitment, and there may be a threat of abduction. Under such circumstances, it is for the local communities to decide whether to send their children to school.

In situations where there is an international peacekeeping force, care must be taken to protect young persons from sexual exploitation and rape. This requires education for peacekeepers regarding their moral obligations, and education for young people on the hazards of unwanted or unprotected sex. This is all the more important given the accelerated spread of HIV/AIDS in many situations of armed conflict. The same considerations apply to all humanitarian and security personnel.

Most protection benefits require an active policy on the part of educators, and are not given automatically. Educational administrators must make great efforts to prevent a deterioration of children's rights, which can occur as a result of ignoring such incidents as bullying, or demands for sexual favours by teachers in exchange for good marks or promotion to the next grade, which is a widely reported occurrence. Codes of conduct for teachers are important, as is the need for strong disciplinary measures against teachers who abuse their position. Students, especially girls, may need protection from the sexual attention of fellow students, rape during transit to and from school, and similar problems.

V. Resources for education in crisis and recovery

Crisis-affected communities provide many of the resources for emergency education, but support from the wider international community is often needed to permit an adequate response. In this chapter we begin by considering the human side of resourcing, i.e. the role of the community and the need for training and capacity-building, before we move on to look at physical resources which are required.

The principle of community participation:
education programmes should use a community-based participatory approach, with emphasis on capacity-building.

In an emergency situation, parents and communities often state that once they have food and shelter, their primary concern is for the resumption of education, and often they set up educational activities themselves. This 'bottom-up' approach is advantageous in several respects and is encouraged by leading assistance agencies. (For examples, see Bird (1999); Brown (2001); Lange (1998); Midttun (1998); Nicolai (2000); Sinclair (2001); Sommers (1999)). There is a psychosocial benefit when community members act as teachers or support the process in other ways. Moreover, there are many situations where the government is unlikely to be able to resource education fully in the longer term, and it is important to educate community members about the ways in which they can support a school and other activities for young people. Good practice for assistance programmes includes:

- establishing school or community/village education committees and youth education/activity committees, and providing training on how to organize and support education and other structured activities for children and young people;
- electing experienced teachers and social workers from the crisis-affected community as headteachers and youth organizers, and providing training for these functions;

- recruiting volunteers from the crisis-affected community as the teachers and youth leaders, and providing training and on-the-job guidance and supervision;
- hiring professionals from the community as project managers and supervisors of NGO assistance projects and providing on-the-job training, leading to increased or full responsibility for project management.

Role of school and youth management committees

Some education programmes promote *School Management Committees, Community Education Committees* or *Village Education Committees,* which include leading members of the community; others promote *Parent/Teacher Associations,* which include all parents and an executive committee. Here, for brevity, we use the term 'committee' to include the various options.

In new *refugee or IDP* situations, there is often support from NGOs and UNHCR's *Community Services Officers* or UNICEF *staff members* for the formation of community/local education committees to help clear spaces for schools and erect temporary shelter, identify volunteer teachers and assess the numbers of students for each year of schooling. The committees also help organize activities for pre-school children and for out-of-school adolescents and youth (although in the past, this has often been delayed). As soon as an education programme has been established, it is important to provide training for the education and youth committees. Some countries, such as Afghanistan, did not have a tradition of such committees, and Afghan refugee headteachers thought it was an interesting idea but didn't quite understand what would be the role of the committee, or were of the opinion that meeting parents when their children have problems is sufficient. UNHCR encouraged agencies working with Afghan refugees in Pakistan to hire community workers to help establish and train school committees in order to lessen dependence on external support, and prepare for a situation after repatriation where schools in remote locations would need to be self-reliant.

In situations of ongoing *conflict, insecurity and instability*, the training of committees in self-management is especially important.

UNESCO's *Programme for Education for Emergency and Reconstruction* (UNESCO-PEER, based in Nairobi) developed the *'Teacher Emergency Package'* (of educational supplies and materials) in Somalia in 1992 so that communities could organize their own schools, despite the absence of the government. UNESCO-PEER saw *School Management Committees* as a way of bringing members of the community together as a force for peace. UNICEF has recently prepared a handbook for schools in Somalia, proposing ways in which communities can improve the quality of the school environment.

The principle of human resource development:
education programmes should include a major component of training for teachers and youth/adult educators, and provide incentives to lessen teacher turnover.

In some displacement situations the teachers move with their communities and can resume their teaching duties. In other situations there is a shortage of experienced teachers, and educated people volunteer as teachers. As an education system is established, or re-established, it is necessary to screen volunteers and to select the best teachers, taking into consideration not only their education and personal qualities, but also the need to reach (or work towards reaching) a target quota of at least 50 per cent women teachers to provide role models and a sense of security for girls attending school.

In many crisis-affected communities, teachers are underqualified and untrained. Even trained teachers may have had limited exposure to modern teaching methods. The focus has been on *'chalk and talk'*, and often on rote learning rather than on comprehension. Crisis may provide an opportunity to introduce a new approach to teacher training which can help even inexperienced teachers to develop the skills required for effective teaching, as well as taking into account the special needs of children exposed to some form of crisis. As noted by Graça Machel (2001), *"fear and disruption make it difficult to maintain an atmosphere conducive to learning, and this can take a grievous toll on school morale. In Palestinian schools, surveys found that many teachers and students had trouble concentrating, particularly if they had witnessed or experienced violence or had family members in prison or hiding".*

Any education programme focused on crisis-affected populations should therefore include a major component of carefully designed training for teachers and headteachers. Training is needed, likewise, for adult educators and youth educators/youth-group leaders. Such training will initially be provided 'in-service', through vacation courses, mobile trainers, and training of mentor teachers in the schools or school clusters, while open and distance learning methods can be implemented later on. In-service training should be structured and recorded in such a way that arrangements can be made for it to count towards qualified teacher status at a later date.

The training should emphasize clearly structured lessons and activities to help children concentrate, and there should be two-way communication to involve them actively in the teaching/learning process. In its simplest form, such communication can include questioning students individually and considerately (girls and boys equally), regarding their comprehension of subject matter and discussion of its implications. This is a big step forward in some countries. In other countries with more experience of activity-based education, there can be more emphasis on small group work. There should be an underlying message of working together to help the society recover from the crisis, with themes such as peaceful resolution of conflicts, citizenship and human rights (including anti-harassment and anti-bullying values and measures).

In *refugee and IDP situations*, it is especially important to provide the opportunity for educated refugees to serve as the teachers and youth workers, since this rebuilds the morale of opinion leaders. It also allows children to develop a feeling of normalcy from having teachers from their own community whose language and ways are familiar to them. Initially, these people serve on a voluntary basis but must later undergo selection tests, after which they should receive compensation (an 'incentive') for their services. This compensation is needed to ensure that teachers are not financially disadvantaged compared to their neighbours who undertake petty trade or labouring work; otherwise, there will be frequent turnover of staff, and the training invested in them will be wasted. (Some staff turnover, which occurs as a result of emigration and the hiring of teachers as staff of external agencies, cannot be avoided.) The level of incentives should be set at a level that is sustainable over the longer term in case the crisis is prolonged.

In some cases, local nationals may seek posts as teachers in refugee schools. This may be appropriate where refugees need to study the local language, or where there is a shortage of secondary school teachers. Problems arise, however, if local teachers are paid salaries much higher than those of refugee teachers. The solution which was implemented in Ngara, Tanzania (1994-1996), was to adopt a single pay scale for all refugee and Tanzanian staff. The payment matrix included a modest pay scale for refugee staff (who also benefited from relief assistance such as food, health care, and shelter), a slightly higher pay scale for locally recruited national staff (to compensate for their not receiving relief assistance), and a significantly higher pay scale for staff recruited from Dar es Salaam, who had higher expenses to meet. In Pakistan, both refugee and national teachers in Afghan refugee schools, managed by the provincial governments, initially received pay according to national scales, but this was not sustainable with donors when the refugee situation continued well into its second decade. In 1995, these schools were handed over to non-governmental agencies and funding for teacher remuneration was reduced.

UNHCR has recommended a gender target of at least 50 per cent female teachers, partly to encourage the enrolment of girls in school by providing for them women who serve as role models and counsellors and who can protect them against abuse. Another consideration was that female teachers might be more likely to remain in the profession, both as refugees and after repatriation, whereas male teachers may have greater labour market mobility and seek better paid work. For these reasons, it may be appropriate to select women as teachers who have a lower level of educational achievement than male candidates do, but who show aptitude for the work.

Another issue concerns the recognition of training provided in emergencies. The *International Rescue Committee*, which supported schools for refugees from Liberia and Sierra Leone who had taken refuge in Guinea, offered extensive in-service training and in-school support to the refugee teachers. The *Ministry of Education* in Liberia subsequently recognized the good performance of returnee teachers, but had difficulty in awarding qualified teacher status, which required completion of a specified training curriculum. A compromise was reached whereby a teacher, having received training while in exile, was awarded a basic level teacher qualification. However, it was observed that projects providing training for refugee teachers should include the elements required for qualified teacher status in the home country and should be well documented.

In areas where refugees live close to local populations and follow a similar curriculum, it may be beneficial to include refugee teachers in local teacher training programmes, and *vice versa*. In Northern Uganda, the NGO *Jesuit Refugee Services* paid for Sudanese teachers to participate in the distance education system of teacher training run by the national authorities, thereby allowing them to obtain qualified teacher status.

Confronted with a situation of insecurity in Somalia, UNESCO-PEER used open learning methods in the 1990s in the form of the *Somali Open Learning Unit* (SOMOLU). This drew on the experience of the *Institute of In-Service Teacher Training*, which had previously operated in Somalia for almost ten years, and of the *Sudan Open Learning Unit* (SOLU). Trainees set their own learning pace and appeared for an examination after completion of 30 course assignments and could then obtain a Certificate of *Basic Teacher Training*. The SOMOLU centres had resident tutors who conducted tutorials for individuals and groups (Retamal and Devadoss, 1998).

In situations of *reconstruction*, it may be difficult to find experienced teachers willing to work in rural areas and/or for the low levels of pay that can be managed by the government, which may have a low tax-base.

Land for public services in Tajikistan

In Tajikistan, *the Agricultural Land Department* agreed to provide each teacher, health worker and water system operator with 0.5 hectares of agricultural land, free of taxes or other charges, for a period of four years, with the possibility of extension if the government is still unable to raise the level of salaries. Other land is set aside to cover the costs of maintenance, furniture and equipment.

Source: UNOPS (2002).

In Liberia in the late 1990s, for example, it was difficult to attract refugee teachers to repatriate and work in Liberian government schools for a salary below the modest incentives they were receiving in Guinea. They were well trained, and on repatriation could easily obtain relatively well-paid jobs in private schools. The Government, therefore, had to recruit educated persons willing to work as teachers in their own districts and provide in-service training. As it happened, educated youth hired on this basis were motivated to work for low pay, because they felt that they were gaining skills from this training and would be considered for full-time training at the teacher education colleges being restored under the rehabilitation scheme (Carl Triplehorn, private communication). For other methods of compensating teachers in reconstruction situations, see *Chapter IX* below.

Teacher training is a major task during the reconstruction phase. The interest of donors at this time should be harnessed to ensure reconstruction of teacher training institutions and enhancing their effectiveness. Such institutions can also be used as centres for in-service vacation courses and as bases for mobile teacher trainers.

The possibility of developing distance learning approaches to countrywide training of teachers should be explored. This can provide a mechanism for training large numbers of untrained teachers simultaneously. This again could attract donor support, since expenditures will be at their highest during the initial development phase when international interest is at its peak.

Distance learning

"Both the Commonwealth and the Francophonie have set up specialist agencies to promote co-operation in distance education: the *Commonwealth of Learning* with its headquarters in Vancouver, Canada, and the *Consortium International Francophone de Formation à Distance*, based in Bordeaux, France. Both agencies provide technical assistance in distance education *and have supported transitional activities.*"

Source: UNOPS (2002).

The issue of recognition of teacher training received in exile has been noted above. A somewhat similar problem in Kosovo is being tackled through a creative approach. During the 1990s, many Kosovar Albanians taught in the 'parallel' (unrecognized) school system. As a transitional measure, the new government will recognize this teaching experience as giving two years' credit towards a new teacher qualification. The teachers will need to complete one more academic year of studies through summer courses, at the end of which they will obtain a *'Bachelor of Teaching'* degree (Ed Burke, personal communication).

In conclusion, both training and on-the-job professional support for teachers and youth workers should be at the heart of any education programme for crisis-affected populations. These populations have to face a difficult future and need the best possible education services. Special attention should be given to the training of headteachers in all the scenarios mentioned, as they have to face unfamiliar and challenging situations and help inexperienced staff to work as a team. It is well known that the well-functioning school is the school with an enthusiastic and skilful headteacher.

The principle of cost-effective and appropriate resourcing:

crisis and recovery programmes should develop and document locally appropriate target resourcing standards, adequate to meet their educational and psychosocial objectives.

The level of resourcing of emergency education programmes needs careful consideration in order to promote sustainability and avoid local rivalries. UNHCR suggests that shelter, equipment and materials standards be developed by reference to the general level of well-run government schools in rural areas near the national capital, rather than the dysfunctional low levels often found in neglected rural areas where refugee camps may be located (UNHCR, 1995).

Assistance agencies are obliged to ensure that their resources do, indeed, lead to the intended results, such as sustainable literacy and numeracy for primary school graduates or success in secondary school examinations, through measures such as requiring regular teacher attendance and supply of teaching/learning materials. This may lead to better results than in local schools. Any such discrepancies should be lead to an effort to improve the local schools. When a large refugee or IDP population moves into an area with weak education systems, then efforts should be made to raise standards in that area for the local population through mobilizing the necessary national and international resources.

The actual standards of resourcing that are appropriate will vary from one situation to another. It is important, however, to specify what the intended standards of resourcing should be, and to have clear plans for working towards them. In 1997, UNHCR issued instructions on minimum standards for the resourcing of refugee schools and began the task of developing country-specific standards. This exercise foundered because it was followed by a funding crisis that lasted several years and led to serious cuts in education budgets. The prototype standards can be seen in the 1997 evaluation report on UNHCR's support to refugee education (UNHCR, 1997b) and in Aguilar and Retamal (1998). A fundamental element was the fact that children need reading practice if they are to become literate, and that textbooks should be distributed to every child, or at least be available in 'class sets' of 40 or 50 that could be used by several different classes. The standards for secondary education require textbooks for all students so that they can compensate for what are often limited hours of schooling and under-qualified teachers. Supplementary reading materials such as library books are also recommended. These standards are met in some UNHCR-supported refugee education programmes, such as those in Pakistan and Nepal, but not in others.

How many books make a library?

The Kigali Model Secondary School, built with support from UNHCR in 1996 and operated by the *Forum for African Women Educationalists* (FAWE), housed 160 students from all parts of the country in 1996, and four teachers. At the last count, the library had 25 books. There is a shortage of textbooks also; the headmistress aspires as a next step to have one textbook per five students!

Source: Machel (2001).

Another key resourcing question is class size. The UNHCR standards seek to limit class size rather than focusing on the student/ teacher ratio. This ratio is very confusing when some classes use a shift system (with either the same or different teachers teaching the morning and afternoon shifts). It is, also, not very useful as an international measure due to variations between education systems. Some systems use a single 'class' teacher throughout primary school, while other systems use 'subject' teachers from an early stage. (The use of subject teachers in primary school in situations of crisis has been justified to the author by the limited subject matter or pedagogic competencies of some teachers, as well as the habitual absenteeism and/or drink problems of particular individuals.)

The lack of basic teaching aids and equipment of almost any kind is a feature of many emergency schools, even when assistance agencies are in a position to introduce good practice. There are many refugee schools managed by international programmes where the only maps or teaching aids available in the school are firmly attached to the walls of the headteacher's room, and where there is no trace of even the simplest science kit or recreational materials. Again, there is a need to prepare targets for low-cost solutions and a plan for implementing them.

Regarding the site planning for emergency schools, UNICEF has developed the concept of 'child-friendly spaces' and 'child-friendly environment'. Child-friendly spaces, in Albania for Kosovo refugees, and in tent cities in Turkey after the 1999 earthquake, meant grouping together basic services for mothers and children, including basic health services, early childhood care and development, schools, recreational facilities, psychosocial support, youth activities and mother support.

Agencies and governments should have a more professional approach to the resourcing of emergency education programmes than simply to authorize a small budget, and turn a blind eye. Resourcing problems, ranging from the lack of textbooks and other reading matter, to the lack of classrooms to protect children from the rain, sun or cold, and of simple recreational equipment, should be registered in the regular statistical monitoring forms and reported systematically to the government(s) concerned, agency headquarters and donors. Often, very little funding can greatly increase cost-effectiveness, but the need is rarely reported to those who are able to provide financial assistance.

Cynics say that so many schools worldwide have resourcing problems, so why should '*emergency schools*' be any different? Some of the answers have been given already, but it is a very important point in connection with resource allocation.

- Children affected by crisis have special needs, including good teaching and learning conditions to help meet psychosocial needs and create a sense of achievement and self-esteem, as well as opportunities for recreation and expressive activities.
- Families affected by conflict may not give their children the normal level of support and stimulus.
- In crisis situations, children, even those from literate families, may be in a print-poor environment.
- Children affected by conflict will later have to help rebuild their communities and need education to do this.

- Schools established in crisis situations *neither* have resources previously accumulated over a period of years *nor* local patrons to meet their needs for special occasions such as sports days.
- Teachers in crisis situations face difficult and unfamiliar situations, are often under-educated and untrained, and require additional support through training and materials.

VI. Special features of education in crisis and recovery

The principle of healing:
all crisis-affected children and young people should have access to education, recreation and related activities, helping meet their psychosocial needs in the short- and longer-term.

Terminology

Problems such as *withdrawal*, *aggression*, and *general depression* or *despair* caused by a crisis are often called 'psychosocial', but this term is controversial. Some professionals use it to refer to the need for individual therapy. Others use it, as in the phrase 'meeting psychosocial needs', to cover problems that are relieved when trauma-affected children and adults are able to engage in social and group activities that restore a sense of normality and relieve tension.

Where there has been acute exposure to traumatic events, the term 'trauma healing' is sometimes used in the sense of meeting the psychosocial needs through organized expressive and physical activities for children and young people.

Psychosocial strains are not merely short-term, but can rise to the surface after several years of normality following a crisis. This should be borne in mind when planning education, recreational, and similar programmes for trauma-affected populations.

As noted in the second section of *Chapter IV*, it is important to meet the basic psychological needs of children and young people affected by conflict (Miller and Affolter, 2002; see also www.ginie.org). This includes helping communities to begin simple education and recreational activities as soon as possible (ISCA, 1996; Lowicki, 2000; UNHCR, 1997a). The first step has often been to establish pre-school and lower primary school classes for the youngest children, which is perhaps the easiest thing to do.

Older children and young people are more aware of the nature and implications of the crisis for their lives, however, and urgently need organized 'structured' activities, including the opportunity to maintain or develop their study skills. This should lead to the opportunity to resume their primary, secondary or tertiary education as soon as possible; or, in the case of out-of-school youth and adults, to participate in non-formal education and informal education linked to recreational, cultural and social service activities.

The *Convention on the Rights of the Child* includes the right to *"engage in play and recreational activities appropriate to the age of the child and to participate freely in cultural life and the arts"*, and requires States Parties to *"encourage the provision of appropriate and equal opportunities for cultural, artistic, recreational and leisure activity" (Article 31)*. This is especially important for crisis-affected children (Tolfree, 1996). Such activities are a necessary part of schooling which supports *"the development of the child's personality, talents and mental and physical abilities to their fullest potential"*, as required by the Convention *(Article 29)*, but are also needed to meet the psychosocial needs of out-of-school young people.

**Implementing education and related provisions
of the *Convention on the Rights of the Child***

The Convention refers to persons under the age of 18 years, but it is neither realistic nor desirable to design education, recreation or cultural programmes specifically for adolescents up to the age of 18 and exclude their natural partners aged 18 to 20 or even 25 years, for example. Hence, the mention in this booklet of programmes for 'young people' refers to programmes for young people aged from 10 to 24 years inclusive, and even some persons in their upper twenties. These programmes should be designed in the light of local conditions and cultures to meet the needs of crisis-affected young people through formal and non-formal education, recreational and cultural activities.

The work of *Save the Children* Sweden and UNICEF with boys who survived a dangerous trek from Southern Sudan to Ethiopia in 1988 who had to return in traumatic circumstances in 1991 and, before moving again to Kenya, helped bring the psychosocial needs of *refugee* children to the fore. Schooling was an integral part of the varied activities organized for this group in Ethiopia and in Kakuma refugee camp in Kenya. In Ngara, Tanzania, the NGO *Norwegian People's Aid* began simple educational and recreational activities for refugee children from Rwanda within two months of their fleeing the 1994 genocide, in which many of their families had been involved. The large Rwandan refugee schools in Tanzania each had a 'psychosocial teacher' who appeared to have beneficial effects on the pupils in these schools.

In some refugee and IDP situations there are different agencies responsible for schooling, vocational training, and community activities, including non-formal education and recreation. In others, both education and community services are supported by the same NGO, as has been the case in most camps for Rwandan and Burundi refugees in Tanzania. Activities undertaken in these camps include reproductive health training and HIV/AIDS awareness for adolescents and youth; support for youth activities such as skills training, language classes, distance education, sports and culture, debates, drama groups and assistance to vulnerable individuals or families; community awareness-raising on sexual and gender-based violence through workshops, drama, dance, music bands and poems; health and skills training for women (UNHCR, 1999).

Meeting psychosocial needs of Somali refugees in Ethiopia

In eastern Ethiopia, the refugee schools, funded by UNHCR, are managed by the national authorities. This formal education programme has been complemented by a UNHCR-funded education programme implemented by *Save the Children Federation/US* providing teacher training, non-formal education for out-of-school youth (literacy, numeracy and survival skills), support to selected Quranic schools, provision of sports equipment and hiring a games instructor in each camp, support to cultural groups (drama, music, poetry) including their role in disseminating health and peace messages, skills training, adult literacy, and training of camp 'associations' (men's, women's and youth committees).

Source: Save the Children Report to UNHCR (2000).

There is often less international presence in *IDP camps and settlements* than there is in refugee situations due to lack of publicity and visibility, lack of funding, lack of permission from the government, or lack of security. In areas where there has been conflict, the psychosocial needs are similar to those of refugees. In 1993, *Save the Children Sweden* worked in an IDP camp near Jalalabad, Afghanistan, for example, to help organize structured activities and to train parents, who were sometimes depressed and passive, in providing emotional support to their children. Again, the *International Rescue Committee* has worked with internally displaced young people in Georgia and Ingushetia, providing them with a range of activities and helping them to re-enter schooling.

In 1999, during times of instability and insecurity, internally displaced and other crisis-affected children in Freetown, Sierra Leone, benefited from a 'rapid response' approach developed by *Plan International* and the UNESCO Institute of Education, Hamburg. This plan was implemented for an initial period of one month, during which pupils attended normal study periods in the mornings and participated in trauma-healing activities in the afternoons. This combination appeared to reduce the symptoms of post-traumatic shock. The *Norwegian Refugee Council* and UNICEF, working in collaboration with the Ministry of Education, Sierra Leone, adopted a similar approach which included activities designed to promote trauma healing in a rapid response course designed to prepare young adolescents for (re-)entry into schooling.

Trauma healing elements of programmes helping children enter or re-enter schooling in Sierra Leone

The *'Rapid Ed'* programme – developed collaboratively in 1999 by Plan International, UNESCO's Institute of Education, Hamburg, and the Sierra Leone Education Ministry – for conflict-affected children in Freetown included half days devoted to literacy and numeracy, and half days devoted to *'trauma healing'*, physical education and corporal expression, art, music, drama and peace education. The initial trauma healing sessions included structured activities, plus clay modelling, songs and music activities, drama and role-playing, local games, culture and dance (one of these activities each morning)

---

and jump rope, throwing and catching balls, athletics, volleyball and football (one of these each afternoon). (See www.ginie.org/countries/sierraleone/index.htm)

Likewise, the *Norwegian Refugee Council*, together with UNICEF and the Ministry of Education, developed a programme to promote the reinsertion into schooling of children aged 10 and over, comprising literacy, numeracy, physical and health education, religious and moral education, peace and human rights education, and trauma healing guidelines for teachers (Mette Nordstrand and Eldrid Midttun, personal communication).

A situation of conflict, insecurity and instability means that even the simplest activities are difficult to organize. Continuation of schooling, whether in school buildings, homes or elsewhere, is in itself a psychological boost. During the long civil conflict in Lebanon, UNICEF promoted morale-boosting activities for children, for example through a children's magazine and through joint summer camps for adolescents from the warring communities.

The rapid return of refugees to Kosovo in 1999, after a brief displacement to Albania and Macedonia among other places, meant that there was still international interest during the early stages of *reconstruction* for the welfare of Kosovar children, including the desire to promote their psychosocial well-being. Psychosocial experts went to Kosovo on brief missions to train teachers on psychosocial issues. Carl Triplehorn, Education Officer of the *International Rescue Committee* in Kosovo, considered that it might have been better to have had educators with psychosocial experience train teachers in how to teach children in post-crisis situations. He suggested the importance of:

Adjustments to lesson planning: since many children in emergency situations have difficulty in concentrating, the lessons should have discrete units and a very specific beginning and end.

Questioning skills: teachers should ask open-ended questions and should encourage the participation of all children, even of those who may be passive and withdrawn due to their experiences.

Appropriate policy on discipline: a less authoritarian and gentler form of discipline should be used where possible, and strategies developed to cope with students who are confrontational as an aftermath of trauma (personal communication).

Recreational and expressive activities are also important for children both in and out of school. Triplehorn worked closely with the Ministry of Youth in Kosovo to systematically develop programmes for youth.

In situations of reconstruction, it is important to build a *positive mindset for the future.* In East Timor, the *International Rescue Committee* worked with young people to develop a range of activities, including 'study circles' for youth, following on a tradition of the student wing of the independence movement. These study circles were supported with materials to promote discussion of the future development of the country and its culture (Nicolai, 2000).

Emergency education in post-independence East Timor

The *International Rescue Committee* used seed money from the Banyan Tree Foundation to establish an emergency non-formal education programme in the Oecusse enclave of East Timor, beginning in November 1999, soon after Independence. Project objectives and activities were:

Objective 1:   To support the organization of community-based structured activities for children and youth that enhance formal school efforts

Activity 1.1:   Facilitate the establishment of the *Oecusse Children's Centre* managed by the local young women's group, offering daily psychosocial activities for the pre-school age group (recreation, music, art, health care).

Activity 1.2:   Organize non-formal education study circles for adolescents and young adults.

Activity 1.3:   Assist in establishing sports activities for children and youth through aiding leadership of the local youth group.

Activity 1.4:   Explore youth's education, skills training and community activity needs to permit future programming.

Objective 2:	To empower local populations by building teacher and youth capacities for work with children and communities.
Activity 2.1:	Through a local NGO partnership, train local project teams to manage day-to-day implementation.
Activity 2.2:	Develop curriculum materials for non-formal education study circle programmes for youth, covering such topics as conflict resolution, Timorese culture, gender.
Activity 2.3:	Plan and develop materials for the teacher-training workshop series, in collaboration with the *District Education Committee.*
Activity 2.4:	Provide technical assistance to youth groups in applying for and securing funds to support their community service and leadership efforts.
Objective 3:	To evidence direct support for Timorese communities through providing education supplies and on-site staff presence.
Activity 3.1:	Procure and distribute education supplies and materials.
Activity 3.2:	Establish a field office with part time presence of education staff.
Activity 3.3:	Provide transportation to local groups in their efforts to support schools or develop programmes for children and youth.

Source: Nicolai (2000).

Resources are needed if students and out-of-school young people are to have access to recreational and expressive activities. In terms of resources, simple recreational materials are now often included in kits of supplies for emergencies. UNICEF sometimes supplies 'recreation kits' as well as education kits from its Copenhagen store. However, since these are quite costly and weigh 35 to 40 kilos each and many of the contents need to be replaced regularly, it is better to develop local sourcing arrangements where possible.

Good practice requires that in emergency situations all teachers – or at least one or two teachers per school – and all youth workers receive urgent training regarding the psychosocial effects of trauma. Teachers should receive at least a guidance pamphlet on how to cope with their own problems and how to adapt their teaching to meet children's needs. Governments and teacher educators working with crisis-affected or disaster-prone populations should incorporate the psychosocial dimension into all teacher-training programmes. This will be useful since, even in peaceful times, there will always be some students who have to cope with the loss of relatives and friends, all the more so in regions heavily affected by HIV/AIDS. It will mean that teachers are better placed to cope with individual students' needs, and also with possible natural disasters or other unforeseen crises.

In *summary*, good practice for education programmes for young people in disrupted societies requires resources to support:

- the involvement of almost all children and young people in education programmes, whether formal or non-formal;
- formal or non-formal skills-based education for health (including HIV/AIDS education), safety, the environment, and conflict resolution/peace/citizenship (see below);
- appropriate sport and recreational activities, catering to females as well as to males, and related training enriched with informal education on the above topics;
- appropriate artistic and cultural activities;
- youth community centres and study circles;
- access to libraries, newsletters produced by young people, etc.;
- other leisure and income-generating activities and related training.

Increasingly, access to computers and electronic communications and related education will feature on such a list.

Co-ordination between organizations providing education, training and community services should ensure that structured activities are available to all crisis-affected young people. Activities not covered by others should be undertaken by the organization(s) supporting schooling, with day-to-day responsibilities delegated as much as possible to young people themselves and to trained youth co-ordinators. Besides meeting the psychosocial needs that arise as a result of the crisis, such activities help in laying the foundations for future citizenship, peace and prosperity.

The principle of curriculum policy oriented to long-term solutions:
curriculum policy should support the long-term development of individual students and of the society, and in refugee populations should be supportive of a durable solution, normally repatriation.

Education sometimes contributes to conflict, as is the case when there are gross discrepancies in education facilities for different social groups, or when the school curricula glorify the nation, or a dominant group within it, and refer negatively to neighbouring countries, particular social groups or the 'enemy'. A time of crisis is an opportunity to review past weaknesses and to develop a modernized and more unifying education programme for the future (Pigozzi, 1999).

Curriculum policy in refugee situations

The principal difference between education for refugees and other crisis-affected people is that refugees are separated from the education system of their own country which has its own curriculum, its own assessment and examination procedures, its own system of progressing from one level of education to the next, and its own approaches to teacher training and certification. When refugees are first displaced, the curriculum in refugee schools is normally that with which teachers and students are familiar: this is both practical and psychologically reassuring. The use of the curriculum of the country or area of origin also helps children re-enter their own education system after repatriation and is known as 'education for repatriation'. If possible, the refugees continue to use home country textbooks and sit home country examinations.

Education for repatriation

Mozambican refugees in Malawi and Zimbabwe followed their home curriculum with the support of their home government. Students were able to repatriate in the early 1990s and reintegrate into their national system. The smaller number of refugees who had settled in other countries had attended schools which followed local curricula through the medium of English and faced problems when they repatriated to Mozambique, where schools use Portuguese as the language of instruction.

The *International Refugee Committee* implemented a large programme of refugee education in Guinea in the 1990s, catering to refugees from both Liberia and Sierra Leone. This NGO developed a refugee school curriculum, which met the needs of both countries of origin. The students were able to sit examinations set by the *West African Examinations Council*, the results of which would be recognized in their home countries.

Education for refugees in Tanzania in the 1990s has been based on the principle of education for repatriation. In recent years, refugees from Burundi and the *Democratic Republic of Congo* have taken school leaving examinations administered by their respective national education authorities, despite instability in their home countries. This was made possible thanks to the continued efforts of the staff of the concerned governments, UNICEF and UNHCR.

Refugees from Southern Sudan, whose educational tradition was through the medium of English, have decided to continue with this type of education (which had been discontinued by the Sudanese Government), in the hope that the tradition will be restored. They have opted to take the national examinations in their host countries of Uganda and Kenya. This has permitted movement from refugee schools to national secondary and/or post-secondary education.

In some situations where refugees expect a long wait before it is safe to return home, it may be possible to use a curriculum that 'faces both ways'. Thus Afghan refugees in Pakistan in the 1980s and 1990s used a version of their home country curriculum but with the added subject of Urdu, the national language of Pakistan.

Reconstruction

Post-conflict reconstruction may be the occasion for a complete review of the curriculum. This is the case in Afghanistan, for example, where there have been over two decades of conflict, during which there was no nationally accepted curriculum. Different curricula were developed during the 1980s for refugee schools and for government-controlled and mujahidin-controlled areas of Afghanistan. In such circumstances, there has to be an interim period when curricula and textbooks from the past are used while urgent efforts are made to develop a national consensus on curriculum policy. A similar phased approach was needed in Kosovo in 1999, where previously two school systems (Serbian and Albanian) had been running side by side, and in East Timor, also in 1999, where the Indonesian curriculum had been in use and a specifically Timorese curriculum had to be developed. The problems of reintegrating separate school systems have been especially difficult in Bosnia Herzegovina.

Problems of curriculum reform in Bosnia Herzegovina

"Efforts are being made by the *Office of the High Representative* in co-operation with other agencies to prevent nationalists using the education system to foster division and to bring together the three parallel education systems. In 2000, the High Representative obtained the agreement of Education Ministers in the *Federation* and the *Republika Srpska* to delete offensive references in textbooks which apportioned blame for aggression and war crimes to 'other sides'. In some municipalities in the Federation the 'two schools under one roof policy' is allowing Bosniak and Croat pupils and teachers to share educational facilities and organize joint extra-curricular activities. In the *District of Brcko*, progress has been made in establishing conditions for multi-ethnic education. Civic education classes discussing human rights are being set up. Efforts are being made to teach both Latin and Cyrillic alphabets and develop language modules which highlight the common linguistic heritage of the three peoples. Yet there has been resistance...(and) most textbooks still refer to obsolete curricula and learning methodologies which can only be addressed through a comprehensive reform which will take up to five years... Substantial and sustained external political pressure has had to be applied to push through these reforms."

Source: Englbrecht (2001).

The textbooks used previously often incorporated hurtful and hateful language about the other party to a conflict. Before reprinting textbooks, the United Nations Mission in Kosovo took measures to remove negative ethnic messages and biased historical references. Care was taken that the editors hired to eliminate any provocative text did not retain negative messages, be it intentionally or unintentionally (Ed Burke, personal communication).

Developing curricula and textbooks takes time. It is important to arrange study visits to bring national curriculum specialists up-to-date with current professional thinking and recent international experience in similar situations. Technical work on curriculum planning and development for the longer term needs to proceed hand-in-hand with countrywide discussion of the key issues, leading to a consensus on curriculum policy.

The principle of curriculum enrichment with life skills for healthy and peaceful living:

education programmes should be enriched to include education for health, safety, environmental awareness, peace/conflict resolution, human rights and citizenship.

Throughout the 1990s there has been a growing awareness of the need for emergency education to convey "supplementary survival messages" (Aguilar and Retamal, 1998). Crises carry health hazards, from displacement into unsanitary and crowded camps to unwanted or unprotected sex with persons infected with HIV/AIDS. There may be dangers from landmines or unexploded munitions. The environment may be damaged as a result of refugees cutting down all trees, within reach of a camp, for shelter and fuel. In the aftermath of civil conflict there is a need to develop skills for peace, for the promotion of human rights and for civic participation. Good practice emergency education programmes ensure that schools and non-formal education programmes enrich their activities with these elements, which are often omitted from traditional subject-focused curricula or treated in a formalistic way that does not impact on children's or adults' behaviour.

Particular attention must be given, at present, to skills-based education for the protection of young people against *HIV/AIDS,* which represents a huge threat to the lives of young people in many countries, all the more so if there has been disruption of protective social structures due to conflict and displacement. There are problems which arise in the teaching of such subjects, since parents often object to explicit education about sexual matters: this should be handled through discussions with community members to find a way of approaching the subject that takes note of local concerns. It is not enough to convey the biological facts, although these should be systematically repeated and erroneous beliefs dispelled. In order to change behaviours, it is necessary to build a repertoire of life skills, from non-violent communication and assertiveness in explaining one's position, to negotiation and conflict management. These behaviours must be practised through repeated role-plays incorporating different ways of saying 'no' to unwanted or unprotected sex (WHO and UNESCO, 1994).

Presenting the dangers of *landmines and unexploded munitions* is a vital part of education in some crisis or post-conflict situations, while in others it is not necessary. For those high-risk areas, there are several good manuals available (Baxter *et al.*, 1997; Save the Children Sweden, 1999; UNICEF, undated; UNHCR and Save the Children Alliance, 2000). Again, it is important to use activity-based approaches, which help children internalize life-saving reactions when faced with mines and other dangerous objects.

Environmental education is specifically mentioned as an obligation under the *Convention on the Rights of the Child* (*Article 29e*), and supplementary resources are needed to enrich its teaching under science and other subjects and/or to separately teach the messages of especial importance in a crisis situation (Talbot and Muigai, 1998). Efforts should be made to raise awareness on natural disasters that occur in the area, including safety measures and ways of lessening impact (e.g. through preserving forests to reduce the effects of floods and help prevent mud-slides) (UNICEF, 1999). Children and adults should be trained in behaviours that can provide protection from environmental disasters, as in the Turkish programme for children in which a character named 'Grandpa Earthquake' gives lessons in appropriate behaviours during earthquakes (IFRC, 2002) or the teachers' workshops in Macedonia which develop possible classroom activities (UNICEF, 1998).

The importance of *education for peace and citizenship* was encapsulated in the remark of a visitor who saw the camps set up in Tanzania to shelter refugees whose community had committed genocide and asked what was being done to help them see their way to a better future. Education for peace and human rights is in fact required by many human rights documents but is often neglected. *Article 26* of the *Universal Declaration of Human Rights* requires that education promotes understanding, tolerance and friendship among all nations, racial or religious groups, and furthers UN activities for the maintenance of peace. This requirement is made binding upon all governments under a similar provision of the *Convention on the Rights of the Child.*

Education for peace and human rights under the *Convention on the Rights of the Child*

"States Parties agree that the education of the child shall be directed to:

...

(b)   The development of respect for human rights...

(c)   The development of respect for ...the national values of the country in which the child is living, the country from which he or she may originate, and for civilisations different from his or her own;

(a)   The preparation of the child for responsible life in a free society, in the spirit of understanding, peace, tolerance, equality of sexes and friendship among all peoples, ethnic, national and religious groups and persons of indigenous origin."

Source: Article 29.

When a population has faced a war or internal civil conflict, there needs to be a process of understanding the causes of conflict and how the cycle of conflict and subsequent hostility or revenge can be brought to an end. In recent years, there have been peace education initiatives supported by UN agencies, ministries of education, international and local NGOs in many conflict or post-conflict situations (Fountain, 1997, 1999; Machel, 2001).

Life skills education oriented towards preserving peace focuses on the inter-personal and relationship skills of non-violent communication, co-operation, negotiation and mediation, and is needed both by children and adults throughout the world. In emergencies, this can help people cope with day-to-day problems arising in their difficult situations and support leaders who pursue peaceful solutions at community and national levels. UNHCR has found an enthusiastic response to its initiative based on this approach among refugees as well as in post-conflict situations (Baxter, 2001; Sommers, 2001; Obura,

2002). Human rights education shows how the values of empathy and respect for others have been codified and agreed upon by governments worldwide (Johannessen, 2002). Citizenship education is closely related to education for peace and human rights, and is especially relevant in post-conflict reconstruction where citizens need to understand the peace agreement or constitutional arrangements and national laws.

Generic elements of education for peace in emergency situations

Peace education uses participative activities and discussion to help develop skills, concepts and values supportive of peace-building (adapted from Baxter, 2000):

CONCEPT AREAS	• *Non-violent communication* • *Appropriate assertiveness* • *Co-operation* • *Critical thinking* • *Conflict resolution* • *Peace* • *Human rights and responsibilities* • *Self-respect and respect for others*
SKILLS	• *Active listening* • *Perceptions and empathy* • *Emotional awareness* • *Bias* • *Stereotypes, prejudice and discrimination* • *Understanding of self and others* • *Similarities and differences* • *Assertion, aggression and submission* • *Strengths and weaknesses* • *Trust* • *Analysis and bias* • *Problem solving* • *Negotiation* • *Mediation* • *Reconciliation*
CONTEXTUAL KNOWLEDGE, VALUES AND ATTITUDES	• *Peace and conflict* • *Universal Declaration, CRC, CEDAW* • *Citizenship, laws and governance* • *Social responsibility* • *Tolerance*

How to organize life skills education in schools

One very important question is whether to attempt the integration of these messages into regular curricula or whether to support special programmes in these areas. Integration is difficult when teachers are inexperienced and under-educated, especially where education is examination-oriented and the examinations focus on theory rather than on contemporary problems. It is not sufficient, for example, simply to provide information about HIV/AIDS. Life skills training is needed on how to say 'no' to unwanted or unprotected sex if behaviour is to change. Moreover, many teachers would be unable or unwilling to conduct participative classes on such a topic. It is preferable, therefore, to allocate specialist teachers to provide skills-based health education in special classes and to youth groups.

UNICEF has examined this issue systematically in connection with HIV/AIDS education. Research has shown that skills-based HIV/AIDS education offered as a separate subject taught by separate teachers is more effective in changing the behaviour of adolescent students than incorporating it into a 'carrier' subject or implementing a policy of infusion into all subjects (Gillespie, 2002).

The same experience was reported by the UNESCO-PEER/UNHCR environmental education programme for refugees in East Africa. Attempts to integrate the new materials into existing school subjects by linking them to practical activities had limited impact. It was too complicated for poorly educated teachers who already had insufficient time and resources to teach the examinable elements of the core school subjects (Chris Taylor, personal communication).

The UNHCR peace education programme, in contrast, used a separate subject approach. They decided to select teachers who had the potential to use participative methods, train them in the necessary course materials and skills, and make peace education their primary responsibility. Where there is not a full time workload, the teacher may teach other subjects in addition to peace education.

It is clear that the enrichment of the curriculum with health and peace-oriented messages and life skills practice requires additional resources in the form of additional teaching time, as well as start-up training costs. The new *Inter-Agency Network for Education in Emergencies* is attempting to reduce start-up costs for peace education by making the UNHCR materials (which are not specifically for refugees) generally available under its own logo. It is hoped to revise these materials so that they incorporate modules focused on HIV/ AIDS awareness, gender awareness, human rights and citizenship, especially for older students.

Resource requirements for a separate subject Life Skills/ Peace Education programme after start-up:

- Trained teacher time of one period per week, per class.
- Trained facilitators to conduct community workshops (part-time, full-time or volunteers).
- Regular vacation training for teachers and facilitators.
- One trainer/supervisor per 10 to 20 schools (depending on distances), plus travel costs.

The principle of vocational training linked to workplace practice:
vocational training programmes should be linked to opportunities for workplace practice of the skills being learned.

There are often demands to divert funds from low-cost education programmes that benefit the many, to skills training programmes that benefit the few and have a higher *per capita* cost. It is often said that unemployed or 'idle' youth in refugee camps or other crisis situations should be given vocational training, as if this will lead them all to full-time employment. Alternatively, it is said that the training will help with reconstruction later. However, the crisis-affected populations are usually poor, and there is often limited purchasing power, and little money for purchasing the goods and services that newly trained carpenters or masons can produce. Also, skill training centres rarely provide sufficient practical and business skills for ex-trainees to develop their skills as employees or take up self-employment. It is often best, therefore, to apprentice young people to practising craftsmen or craftswomen to learn practical and business skills which are needed in the real world (Avery et al., 1996; Lyby, 2001). This is all the more important in crisis situations where work opportunities are likely to be in the informal sector, rather than based on certificates. Such training can be included during or on completion of a course based in a training centre if preferred. Another option is to channel the production of goods and services needed by assistance programmes, such as school furniture and buildings, into a production unit attached to a training centre, and to employ ex-trainees.

Employment of ex-trainees

A study of the employment of Afghan youth who had attended conventional vocational training centres in Baluchistan, Pakistan, in the 1980s, showed that a very small percentage were able to gain employment or become self-employed using their skills. Studies of a sponsored apprenticeship programme for Afghan refugees in North West Frontier Province, Pakistan in the early 1990s showed that a majority of the ex-trainees were in employment that used their skills.

Source: Sinclair (1988).

It is useful, likewise, to link training in technical or office skills to work experience opportunities with assistance organizations and other employers. It may be noted that reconstruction programmes need supervisors and book-keepers and that these skills should feature in training and work experience programmes, providing an opportunity for secondary school leavers to gain skills that utilize their educational attainments.

In order to provide beneficial structured activities for large numbers of unemployed young people, it is more cost-effective to offer low-cost training in language skills (literacy in the mother tongue, or study of the international languages used in the locality), which can enhance general employability as well as self-esteem. It is also important to consider low-cost training in sports, cultural activities, social service (including peer mediation) and so on, that can help young people to cope with a disrupted living situation (Lyby, 2001).

VII. Co-ordination and capacity-building

The principle of inter-agency co-ordination and co-operation:
governments and assistance agencies should promote co-ordination between all agencies and stakeholders.

In crisis situations there is often a lack of co-ordination, with education programmes being conducted independently by different external and local agencies. Education co-ordination committees are needed at local- and national-level, led by the government and/or the relevant UN agency. In the case of refugees, there should ideally be co-ordination between governments and agencies operating in the country of origin and all major countries of asylum.

Inter-agency co-operation in emergency education response

"An inter-agency team should be formed as soon as possible, under the leadership of either the designated lead agency or the local government to facilitate co-ordinated response, and to reach agreements on critical issues such as:

- Minimum qualifications for teachers and paraprofessionals.
- Common policy on teacher 'incentives'.
- Transparent processes for teacher selection.
- Joint projects, where possible, requiring agencies to exploit their comparative advantages.
- Involvement of civil society, local and international NGOs.
- Sharing of resources for teacher training and curriculum materials development."

Source: UNICEF (2001).

In refugee situations, the natural co-ordination mechanism is through UNHCR, jointly with the government, although UNICEF may undertake this role in large emergencies. For crisis-affected populations within their own country, emergency co-ordination is normally through the government, assisted by UNICEF. In this instance, UNHCR may provide support for education in regions receiving returning refugees.

Co-ordination mechanisms

In Uganda in the 1990s, UNHCR and the Government hosted quarterly meetings of all agencies concerned with refugee education to discuss policy issues of current concern and also a selected topic of common interest.

In Peshawar, Pakistan, in the 1980s and 1990s, the *Education Cell* of the provincial *Commissionerate for Afghan Refugees* hosted a monthly meeting of all agencies concerned with refugee education. In the 1990s, all Peshawar-based NGOs implementing education programmes for refugees in Afghanistan met monthly at the *Education Sub-Committee* of the NGO co-ordination group, the *Agency Co-ordination Body for Afghan Reconstruction* (ACBAR), to ensure good communications and avoid wasteful duplication.

"The establishment of *Local Education Councils* (representing all stakeholders) is the cornerstone initiative to reinforce local capacities for reconciliation, consensual agreement and decentralization."

Source: UNOPS (2002).

The principle of capacity-building:
external assistance programmes should include capacity building to promote transparent, accountable and inclusive system management by local actors.

There are exceptional demands on educational planners, managers and administrators at times of crisis and reconstruction. National ministries and district education offices need support in terms of equipment, transport and staff training in order to cope with their additional duties and to co-ordinate external assistance, if this is forthcoming.

It is important for international NGOs to train their management staff to progressively take over the running of programmes as a step towards sustainability, and possibly in the creation of a local NGO to become its own successor. Effective programmes develop profiles of staff skills and required training. International agencies and donors can help build the capacities of local NGOs through core financing, staff training, and funding partnership arrangements with international NGOs. Some NGOs, such as the *International Rescue Committee*, have been known to run 'umbrella' projects, providing funding to a number of local NGOs.

The training of supervisors and trainers is important. The *Swedish Committee for Afghanistan*, an NGO working in many parts of Afghanistan since the 1980s, has introduced a system of distance learning for field supervisors and trainers, with assignments set and marked by educators in Sweden who have previously worked on the NGO's programme.

In reconstruction situations, the task of managing the core education programmes falls to national- and district-level government officials. It is desirable to develop mechanisms, possibly including self-study materials, for training district level education officers, since there may be frequent turnover of staff and reconstruction will take years to achieve. This is all the more important if reconstruction is seen as an opportunity to modernize and improve the structure of the education system and the quality and content of the education provided.

The strengthening of local capacity for the planning and management of education systems and projects is often overlooked in the haste to establish programmes that reach children, adolescents or adults. Capacity-building is crucial for the sustainability of the benefits intended, however.

Building local capacity for literacy services in Guatemala

Comunidades Mayas Alfabetizadas (COMAL) is a *Women's Adult Literacy and Community Development Program* funded through a *USAID Co-operative Agreement*, part of the Guatemalan Peace Accords, and currently being implemented by *Save the Children Federation/USA* and a network of 16 national NGOs. The principal aim of COMAL is to leave a tested and working adult education system targeted at women and youth in the hands of local civic groups and NGOs working in close contact with Mayan communities trying to reconstruct their society after a devastating 30-year civil war.

Source: Dall (2001).

VIII. Applying these principles: the government perspective

As noted above, the principles set out in *Chapters IV to VII* are not very different from the principles of good education programmes in general. However, practitioners have found them to be especially important in emergency situations. Much of the discussion on good practice has taken place in a series of international seminars and consultations from 1999 to the time of writing, attended mainly by representatives of international NGOs and UN agencies. However, national governments can use these widely accepted principles to guide their response in situations of crisis or reconstruction. In *Chapters VIII and IX*, we look at different situations from the viewpoint of a national government affected directly or indirectly by conflict or disaster. It is not necessary to repeat the principles in detail, and the emphasis here is on additional points to bear in mind.

We look first at special issues related to the governments' preparedness for and response to natural disasters. We then examine the issues of hosting refugees, receiving returning refugees, instability, and finally reconstruction. There is an overlap between these categories, but for purposes of exposition they are treated separately.

The government perspective: disasters

Almost all governments face the consequences that disasters have on education to a greater or lesser extent, for example local floods or high winds. In some cases, there is major damage caused to the entire education system.

Damage to education caused by Hurricane Mitch in Honduras

"In October 1998, Hurricane Mitch left hundreds of thousands of people in Honduras without homes, and destroyed schools, day care centres and entire villages. Approximately 25 per cent of schools were destroyed. Over 250,000 children at primary level and 30,000 at secondary level had their

---

studies drastically interrupted until March 1999. Community day-care and pre-school centres were destroyed or damaged, and around 75,000 children were left without attention. In addition, the central offices of the *Ministry of Education*, located in Comayaguela, were severely damaged. More importantly, the bulk of the education archives were lost and with it the institutional memory of the Ministry. It will take several decades to reconstruct the educational sector in Honduras."

Source: UNICEF (1999).

Preventive safety measures

Education managers can promote safety by designing schools and other educational buildings to meet locally appropriate standards for resistance to earthquakes, climatic hazards such as hurricanes/cyclones, and floods. This entails locally appropriate designs for new permanent and semi-permanent buildings, and long-range planning to convert the stock of older buildings to meet national safety standards; together with supervision to ensure that standards are met. Another important preventive measure is to check on the history of the site selected for the construction of a school to find out if the area has been subject to floods in the past.

Disaster preparedness

From the educational viewpoint, preparedness can include:

* having safe copies of curricula, textbooks, teaching aids and teacher guides (e.g. keeping a complete set in the Education Ministry, complete sets in other specified locations and electronic copies on CD-ROMs, including one lodged with UNESCO's *International Bureau of Education* in Geneva and one at the UNICEF regional office);
* maintaining an updated register of teachers, their qualifications, years of service (for pension entitlements) and area of residence (with electronic or hard copies stored in more than one location);

- developing national guidelines on safe building structures related to locally occurring hazards and local building techniques, and training Ministry and field staff in their application;
- promoting environmental education on natural hazards as part of a culture of disaster prevention and environmental protection in schools and teacher-training programmes, together with safety advice;
- including training on psychosocial needs after trauma, and ways of meeting them, in teacher-training programmes;
- building expertise in disaster response among university faculty members and senior educators, and involving them in disaster response, including monitoring and 'real time' evaluation; and development of expertise through assisting with practical and psychosocial response to small-scale disasters, for example local floods;
- inclusion of education in the national disaster preparedness strategy;
- inclusion of disaster preparedness and response in the national education plan and budget.

Disaster response and post-disaster recovery

Disaster response may involve providing access to education for internally displaced populations or for populations who are in their home areas but have suffered destruction of homes, schools etc. The task of recovery from a large-scale disaster has similarities to the task of post-conflict reconstruction (see below), but the context is more straightforward. There is sympathy for the victims of a disaster, whereas there are internal divisions to heal in the aftermath of civil conflict. It is important to develop both a short-term and a medium-term plan for recovery while there is public and/or international interest and sympathy, *encouraging* a development-oriented *rather than* a relief approach, and giving priority to donors and agencies who are willing to commit resources for the medium-term.

The government perspective: hosting refugees

Hosting refugee camps or settlements represents a challenge for governments, who have to cope with political repercussions and with the management and co-ordination of refugee assistance programmes. It is important that the government establishes appropriate and clear structures for dealing with refugee education. Refugee affairs often come under a home affairs ministry, but there are advantages to having the direct involvement of the education ministry. This can help in teacher training and curriculum issues – especially if the refugee students use the same language of studies – and in planning for government takeover of refugee education infrastructure when the refugees leave.

Important education issues for governments hosting refugees include:

Access

- Ensuring refugee access to institutions in the host country, at primary, secondary or tertiary levels, without discrimination and at fees similar to those of nationals.
- In refugee camps and settlements, promoting rapid response on an 'emergency' basis without delays caused by long-term considerations about curriculum etc. (which can be dealt with later).
- Ensuring that services are provided, whether by the government or by NGOs, in all refugee locations, not merely the conveniently accessible ones; and that common policies are adopted regarding teacher remuneration/incentives, curriculum etc.
- Making arrangements for the studies undertaken in refugee schools and training courses to be recognized, preferably both within the host country and, through diplomatic efforts jointly with concerned UN agencies, within the country of origin.
- Promoting inclusion, with support from national organizations for persons with disability and youth organizations such as the Girl Guides and Boy Scouts.

- Protection of refugee children and adolescents, including limiting the access of militias to refugee schools for recruitment purposes.

Resources

- Promoting the participation of the refugee community in organization and management of refugee education and recreation programmes; including resisting political pressure to turn the refugee education programme into a 'jobs for nationals' venture. Refugees need to be the main actors (teachers, trainers, and managers) as part of capacity-building for repatriation and reconstruction, as well as for psychosocial reasons.
- Making arrangements for the recognition of in-service teacher training of refugees: for recognition both within the host country and, through diplomatic efforts jointly with concerned UN agencies, within the country of origin.
- Making arrangements for refugee teachers to participate, where language usage permits, in national teacher-training programmes.
- National capacity building: seeking funding so that education and other staff of national universities and government educational institutes can get involved in the refugee education programme at the level of needs assessment, monitoring and 'real time' evaluation; and can build national expertise through study tours, fellowships, internet access for networking, etc.
- Strengthening national NGOs through involving them in, or associating them with, refugee education programmes and/or refugee/local joint programmes, and ensuring that they benefit from capacity-building training for refugee staff.
- Promoting donor support for local schools and colleges, and capacity-building for district education offices in refugee-affected areas in order to lessen local resentment of refugees and to help compensate for environmental and other losses incurred by host communities.
- Preparing an inventory of refugee school premises and furniture/ equipment, and plans for takeover and security of these assets when refugees repatriate so that they can be used in local education programmes.

Activities/curriculum

- Supporting the development of refugee education programmes oriented to long-term 'durable' solutions, often through 'education for repatriation' (curricula based on those of the area of origin of the refugees or including the essentials of these curricula).
- Supporting the development of refugee education programmes that meet the psychosocial needs of children and adolescents and promote health, safety, environmental awareness, and skills of conflict-resolution and citizenship.
- Promoting harmonious refugee/local relationships (including shared youth activities, such as sports, where practicable).

Co-ordination and capacity building

- Mobilizing international resources and expertise to help in meeting human rights obligations for refugee education. In some instances, global television coverage leads to widespread international support, but in others support is insufficient or declines rapidly.
- Strong co-ordination of the NGOs and donors offering assistance to ensure a coherent programme; if necessary, asking for an emergency education expert to be deputed to the Ministry to help with co-ordination and to build up expertise of national counterparts; including the establishment of refugee education co-ordination committees at national- and local-level.
- Participating in joint needs assessment and programme design together with concerned UN agencies, NGOs and refugee educators and leaders, including women (ensuring that programme design meets the principles or standards outlined above).

The government perspective: refugees arrive home

Refugees may return home to a well-functioning country or to a country which has suffered large-scale disruption and destruction of infrastructure. The national government may act favourably towards them or regard them as belonging to a less favoured ethnic, religious or political group. Citizens who did not go into exile may regard them as having opted to side-step years of suffering in the home country.

The obligations of the government under the *Convention on the Rights of the Child* and other human rights instruments, mean that every effort must be made to provide returnee children with access to education, rapidly and without discrimination.

Preparatory tasks: building links with concerned refugee educators and NGOs working with refugees prior to repatriation

If the government is actively hostile towards the groups who have become refugees in neighbouring countries, it is unlikely that there will be any preparatory work for repatriation until there are moves towards a peace treaty or something similar. Where the government is willing to do so, however, it can support the education of its citizens who have crossed the border through providing textbooks and educational materials (in bulk or for copying) and arranging the assessment and certification of refugee students' achievements and teacher training.

Ideally, it would be best if the government could become familiar with the NGOs or other organizations that are supporting the education of their citizens living in refugee camps and settlements in neighbouring countries. If these NGOs are efficient, they can play a helpful role in the early stages of post-conflict reconstruction. NGOs can help strengthen district education offices and promote educational reconstruction and development in returnee areas; preferably working in the home areas of the populations they worked with previously.

Re-integration of returning refugees

Important education issues for governments receiving returning refugees include:

Access

•   Ensuring that returnees have rapid access to education, at primary, secondary or tertiary levels, and without discrimination.

- Ensuring that international NGOs work in the areas where they are most needed and that common policies are adopted regarding teacher remuneration/incentives, etc.
- Promoting inclusion and gender equity: returning families may face problems of poverty and insecurity, and special measures are needed to ensure that girls, children with disability, ex-combatants and other special groups are able to participate in schooling.
- Promoting protection and assuring that returnee children and adolescents do not face discrimination and harassment.

Resources

- Promoting the participation of the community in the organization and management of education and recreation programmes with an emphasis on training *School Management Committees* and *Parent/Teacher Associations*.
- Hiring returnee teachers without discrimination, making arrangements for recognition of in-service teacher training received while in exile, and providing in-service training for teachers in returnee areas.
- Strengthening the provincial and district education offices in areas of return, as part of international assistance programmes by governments or NGOs.
- Seeking funding for education and other staff of national universities and government educational institutes to get involved in returnee education programmes at the level of needs assessment, monitoring and 'real time' evaluation; and follow-up with requests to build national expertise through study tours, fellowships, internet access for networking, etc.
- Strengthening national NGOs through involving them in, or associating them with, returnee education programmes, and ensuring that they benefit from capacity-building training organized by government or international NGOs.

Activities/curriculum: similar to those for reconstruction (see below), with emphasis on promoting harmonious returnee/non-returnee relationships.

Co-ordination and capacity building

- Strong co-ordination of NGOs and donors offering assistance to ensure a coherent programme; if necessary, asking for emergency education expert(s) to be deputed to the Ministry or provincial education offices to help with co-ordination and to build up expertise of national counterparts.
- Ensuring that political factors do not lead to under-resourcing of education in returnee areas (international organizations and donors should also be on the lookout for this).
- Participating in joint needs assessment and programme design for education in areas receiving returning refugees, together with concerned UN agencies, NGOs and community educators and leaders, including women (ensuring that programme design meets the principles or standards outlined above). Care should be taken to avoid separate treatment for returnees; programmes should target everyone who lives in the towns and villages concerned.

Special issues concerning the recruitment, training and payment of teachers

In some returnee situations, the returning community has to recreate its own institutions, as the area had previously been totally vacated. In others, returnees rejoin communities that had continued to function in their absence.

It may happen that the government is able to pay teachers, and that the main issue for returning teachers is that they should be eligible for recruitment without discrimination. In other circumstances, the government may have little presence and less budget to pay teachers. In this case, there are a number of approaches to attracting experienced or new teachers to staff schools in the returnee areas. Some examples are cited in *Chapter V* above and *Chapter IX* below. In general, however, schooling in returnee locations will require hiring educated local persons who have no previous teaching experience, and provision of in-service training. Such recruitment should give especial emphasis to female candidates who may be more likely to stay in the area over the longer term, even if they start from a lower educational level than male candidates do. NGOs who have worked with refugees may be willing and able to train these teachers, support district education offices, and raise funding from international donors for such purposes.

Role of UNHCR

UNHCR is required by its statute to protect refugees and assist them in finding durable solutions. Since the 1990s, UNHCR has interpreted this to include helping communities comprised of, or receiving, returnees for a period of about two years after their return. This may include short-term funding for educational activities. Governments sometimes ask UNHCR for expensive educational buildings in favoured locations, but the top priority should be the rapid restoration of schooling in all returnee locations, beginning with plastic sheeting, blackboards, student kits, textbooks etc. Funding may also be sought for in-service teacher training, for strengthening district education offices, and for the restoration of any teacher-training institutions in returnee districts. UNHCR may be willing to fund NGOs to help establish or strengthen schooling in returnee areas during periods of transition.

The government will probably receive assistance from UNICEF for basic schooling (primary and sometimes early secondary school) and early childhood development, whereas UNHCR is focused on promoting durable solutions and can assist the government with any educational activity that fits this description. A government which needs education resources for post-primary education may, therefore, be advised to approach UNHCR at the earliest possible date with well-prepared proposals for education assistance related to the re-integration of returnees, and particularly including assistance which lies outside the mandate or local priorities of UNICEF. The proposal could emphasize that the proposed activities will assist in stabilizing the country and restoring economic activity, such that any risk of a huge influx of refugees recurring in future will be reduced.

Multilateral organizations, such as development banks or the *European Union,* move more slowly than UNHCR and UNICEF. The government should, therefore, begin negotiations for longer-term funding from these latter organizations for development expenditures (infrastructure, curriculum reform and textbook production, etc.) as soon as possible. This may help avoid a '*relief-development gap*' when UNHCR withdraws due to expiry of its mandate, and UNICEF finds that donors' attention is focused elsewhere.

The government perspective: facing intermittent conflict, insecurity and instability

Situations of instability vary greatly and it is difficult to generalize on government response, except to recommend that the principles suggested in this booklet be followed wherever possible.

In some situations, it is difficult to support even the most basic educational operations. Examples include a range of circumstances such as:

- large countries with a poorly developed communications infrastructure, where conflict or security problems mean that areas can be cut off from the ministries of education for months or even years, with little or no advance notice. Here, building local capacity is especially important;
- cities or small geographic areas affected by conflict where concentrated efforts can be made to support home-based or similar educational arrangements.

Under such conditions, brainstorming to create adaptability and flexibility would be advantageous. Some areas, perhaps in and near the capital city, may be administered normally, while others may require special approaches.

Access

- Making travel to school easier and safer through providing escorts for groups of children or by shortening distances through the use of feeder schools for young children, allowing primary schools to add supplementary lower secondary classes etc.
- Asking teachers to compensate for school closures by teaching during what would normally be vacation.

- Facilitating home-based studies (see below) for periods of school closure.
- Rapid re-supplies of schools, which have lost their equipment and materials due to conflict or robbery.
- Use of media, notably radio, to encourage families to send their children to school –including girls – and to promote educational, recreational, cultural and social service activities led by young people.
- Protecting children by closing schools if there is a significant danger that the schools will be attacked, the children abducted, or if the journey to and from school is dangerous.

Resources

Strengthening the motivation and management capacities of School Management Committees

If there is limited and irregular support from central government due to insecurity and conflict, it is important that *School Management Committees* and *Parent/Teacher Associations* are well trained in providing the necessary support to the school. This training should be actively pursued when access is possible, supported by user-friendly handbooks and motivational materials, radio programmes and other media.

■ *Motivation and training of teachers, youth workers and supervisory personnel*

When there is only intermittent contact with field staff, the quality of education depends on their motivation and competence. It is of great importance, therefore, to maximize in-service training of teachers, so that they can continue to work effectively when cut off from normal support. The training of headteachers and senior teachers as 'mentors' who can provide in-school support to newly trained or untrained teachers is also especially important in these circumstances. Another measure which can help teachers is to be sure that all schools or teachers have access to complete sets of textbooks and teacher guides (replaced when necessary), and to provide handbooks and motivational materials for field trainers, supervisors, headteachers and teachers.

■ *Training of teachers, communities and students in child-to-child education*

Given the possible interruption of schooling due to hostilities or teacher turnover, it is important to train teachers and communities in the methods of child-to-child education and to supervise its introduction. This concept has been publicized in developing countries mainly as a means of conveying health messages to families. Child-to-child teaching in support of basic schooling happens naturally in families, but depends on the availability of materials and of older educated children. The methods of child-to-child tutoring could be introduced by education managers as a tool to achieve better school results (and reduce the level of drop-out) even in times of normality. Children could then be asked to undertake such teaching when schooling is interrupted as a form of social service.

■ *Building an expert cadre of concerned educators, including in the diaspora*

When there is conflict or instability, many professionals leave the country to avoid civil conflict, to provide a better future for themselves or their families, and also because in some situations, educated persons are targets for attack. Some professionals migrate to the developed countries and begin a new career there, adding to their knowledge and experience. Often they would like to contribute to the current or future welfare of their homeland, but have little opportunity to do so. It may be useful to establish a network of recognized professionals outside the country, including those who have moved to developed countries and those who may be working with refugee populations in neighbouring countries. This network can be a valuable resource, during and after the conflict. Discussions about future educational development can take place over the internet. Officials in the home country could take part in at least the less political aspects of such discussions, such as the potential advantages of the use of new technologies for reconstruction.

In some circumstances, the network could provide support to educators inside the country or in refugee schools, providing educational materials related to school/university curricula or teacher methods, and even long-distance tutoring for students and for schoolteachers seeking to advance their knowledge and qualifications.

■　*Getting supplies and education materials to users*

One of the problems faced by education programmes in unstable situations is lack of regular access to educational supplies. Some agencies have solved this by sending classroom kits of materials packed in a lockable metal trunk. UNICEF kits come in metal trunks wrapped in thick packaging and with heavy-duty bindings, for example. They weigh about 35 kilograms and are not as easily stolen as small cardboard cartons of pens, scissors, notebooks and so on. UNICEF Somalia has developed specifications for kits, which are sent from Nairobi, needed to start new classes in each of years one to four of schooling. The *Norwegian Refugee Council* and UNICEF have been sending '*Teacher Emergency Packages* (TEPs)' to TEP schools in conflict-affected areas of Angola. Disadvantages of the kits include the need to replenish different items at different rates, and also the need to share scarce items between many classes and schools (meaning that the kits may have to be unpacked at the district level rather than in the classrooms to which they are destined).

■　*Use of open and distance learning*

Some types of open and distance learning can be introduced despite instability, such as educational radio. The *British Broadcasting Corporation* (BBC), in conjunction with UNESCO, produced education programmes for Afghans living in Pakistan and Afghanistan. UNICEF supported an educational newsletter for children during the civil war in Lebanon. Palestinian educators developed self-study materials for use during prolonged closure of the schools.

Activities/curriculum

•　Continuing normal national education programmes and promoting recreational, cultural and social service programmes for out-of-school young people.

- Enriching education programmes with health, safety, environmental and peace messages as much as possible, and reinforcing these messages with non-formal and informal (e.g. radio) programmes for children and youth.
- Informing parents of ways in which they can support their children's education when schools are not functioning, at least by asking them to read aloud to them, and through encouraging child-to-child tutoring.
- Supporting formal education through the use of radio and other media resources (see above).

Co-ordination and capacity building

Co-ordination and capacity building are difficult under insecure conditions. Government efforts to co-ordinate activities and provide security for education programmes in conflict-affected areas will assist national educators and encourage external support.

IX. The government perspective: facing reconstruction

The task of reconstruction proceeds in phases, beginning with emergency response and needs assessment and finally merging into the normal educational development process. Priorities include the strengthening of the ministries of education, the initiation of a national dialogue on educational policy, needs and resources assessment, mobilization of external resources including avoiding the 'relief-development' gap, and co-ordination of national and international actors. The government has to develop a short-term or transitional plan for immediate action, and a medium-term plan for educational reconstruction and development.

Reconstruction issues in Afghanistan

"Consultations with Afghan educators and other stakeholders during this preliminary assessment indicate that the development of a long-term vision and a national education policy are immediate priorities. The national education policy, medium-term plan and strategy should address some of the following key areas:

- *Decentralization:* identification of which powers can be decentralized to which levels.
- *Governance:* determination of policy authority of key stakeholders.
- *Institutional models:* mix of government, state-subsidized, semi-private and private.
- *Public/private partnerships:* role in governance, extent of private sector involvement and accountability in service delivery, construction.
- *Community role in:* resource mobilisation, school governance, access/ quality monitoring.
- *Equity:* gender parity in enrolment, equity in enrolment and achievement.
- *Teaching force:* level of qualifications, competence, status and remuneration.
- *Technical and vocational training:* degree of flexibility and relevance, and market linkage.
- *Tertiary:* degree of autonomy, linkage to private sector, balance of research and teaching."

Source: Asian Development Bank, World Bank, UNDP (2001).

Restoration of the functioning of the Ministries of Education and their regional and local offices

Conditions for post-conflict recovery and reconstruction differ widely (Arnhold et al., 1998; DANIDA, 1996; Dykstra, 2002; Retamal and Aedo-Richmond, 1998; Rugh, 2001; Sommers, 2002). In some instances, for example in Mozambique in the late 1980s and early 1990s, the *Ministry of Education* functions continuously throughout the conflict, and the breakdown in educational administration affects provinces or districts outside the capital city. In other instances, the entire system of educational administration has collapsed and the Ministry may be empty, looted or physically destroyed. Likewise, natural disasters may affect the Ministry itself and much of the country or particular locations.

Re-establishment of educational administration in Afghanistan

In Afghanistan after the defeat of the Taliban Government in late 2001, the *Ministry of Education* was left without furniture, equipment, materials, or services. It was not even clear who was on the staff, though large numbers claimed to have been employed by one of the successive regimes that had overthrown its predecessor. Many of the qualified professionals in the country had emigrated or become refugees. There was little information regarding the status of provincial education offices. A first step was to hold a meeting in Kabul in February 2002, bringing the provincial education directors to Kabul to meet the Education Ministers, aid agencies and each other, and to discuss the problems of reopening the schools, including schools for girls, which the Taliban had closed in 1996. UNICEF deployed a team of education experts to help the Government organize the reopening of schools in time for the new school year in March 2002 under a *Back to School Campaign* involving the distribution of 7,000 tons of education supplies.

Steps needed to restore the functioning of a ministry of education in a post-conflict situation may include:

- selection of up-to-date and committed experts to head and staff the different sections of the Ministry;

- obtaining basic furniture, office and communications equipment (with generators), required means of transport, and supplies to start work quickly;
- solving the problem of staff salaries, through donor support if necessary;
- reaching a temporary solution to the problem of teacher remuneration;
- quick survey and analysis (needs and resources assessment) of the conditions and functioning of schools and other educational institutions;
- emergency supply of school materials, textbooks and simple materials for simple shelter arrangements or repairs (e.g. plastic or nylon sheeting);
- strengthening the educational planning and development unit with donor support, and setting up a simple *Education Management Information System* (EMIS) database (including one or more seconded experts, if needed);
- establishing a mechanism for co-ordination of incoming assistance and for developing project proposals and donor liaison;
- training for concerned officials in budgeting and finance and in management of the education workforce, and developing projects to establish modern systems of personnel and financial management;
- establishment of a task force for renewal of curricula and textbooks, training of concerned staff in modern curriculum development and preparation of project proposals for preparation of new curricula and development, experimenting and introduction of a new generation of textbooks;
- establishment of a task force for renewal of teacher training, including accelerated pre-service training and in-service training structured to lead to a recognized teaching qualification; preparation of project proposals for training of trainers and for rehabilitation and modernization of teacher-training institutions (ensuring, if appropriate, collaboration to promote literacy, language and life skills studies by technical and vocational students, and skills training linked to literacy programmes);
- establishment of a task force for the renewal of higher education, training of concerned ministry and senior university staff, and

formulation of projects for reconstruction and modernization of higher education institutions;

- strengthening the ministry units concerned with primary, secondary and early childhood education, conducting a status review of field education offices, formulating project proposals for their reinstatement and upgrading (through infrastructure repair, staff selection and training, supply of equipment and materials and means of transport (vehicles, motor cycles, bicycles, horses/mules)), so that they can promote and manage the task of educational reconstruction at field level (including donor and NGO co-ordination);
- strengthening the ministry units concerned with school infrastructure through staff training, development of guidelines for short-term and longer-term use regarding appropriate and disaster-resistant buildings, and close liaison with agencies providing external assistance to ensure that these guidelines are respected.

Consensus-building on national education policy

The situation of conflict may have arisen from social divisions reflected in differences of educational opportunity. This was a factor contributing to the civil conflict in Sierra Leone. The conflict may have been followed by an uneasy peace with educational implications as in Bosnia, where it was decided that each canton should develop its own Ministry of Education and where there was political pressure for separate curricula for Serbs, Muslims and Croats. It is desirable to bring together leading educators and intellectuals to discuss the key issues of education policy and move towards a consensus on viable options for educational policy which are supportive of peace building and development. Depending on local circumstances, it may be useful to establish an advisory board of senior educators to provide impartial advice to the Ministry, or to establish time-limited task forces to examine specific issues. However, after a long conflict, these senior persons may be elderly men lacking vision, and it would be best to include young national educators with recent international experience.

Role of regional and local education authorities

In some post-conflict situations, there is an immediate structural problem regarding the role of central and local government in the field of education. Many education administrators recommend decentralization of administrative authority, financial authority, pedagogical and curriculum design authority, etc. It must be questioned whether this is a good idea in situations where a country has suffered recent civil conflict. There is a need to build a shared sense of national identity within a context of international co-operation, rather than the fragmentation seen in Bosnia. On the other hand, there may be a case for some curriculum flexibility, as in the Ixil region of Guatemala, a former conflict zone. Studies have shown that the Mayan children have a poor self-image and have difficulty in commencing schooling as they are taught from the beginning in Spanish rather than in their mother tongue (UNOPS, 2002).

Decentralization of administration and teacher training in Nicaragua

In 1993, the Ministry of Education in Nicaragua created *Municipal Education Councils*, with administrative and financial responsibility for the schools. The Councils were composed of representatives from the private sector, parents, teachers, government officials and community leaders. There was also decentralization of administration within some municipalities to primary and secondary schools. There was de-concentration of authority to 19 regional offices of the Ministry, including budgeting, accounting, logistics, training and evaluation. A USAID-funded project supported extensive training for Ministry staff in these areas, and the creation of an education management information system, facilitating communication between central and local offices.

Under the teacher training component, the project supported the creation of 700 local centres, through which the in-service training of primary school teachers was decentralized.

Source: Cecilia Otero, cited in UNOPS (2002).

It is important to include the question of centralization or decentralization of the various aspects of educational management and programmes as part of the national dialogue to create a consensus to guide the reconstruction plan for education. Although decentralization of administration has the advantage of apparently increasing responsiveness to local conditions and efficiency, care must be taken that this does not provide a foothold for divisive approaches or curricula that threaten to increase ethnic tension.

Needs and resources assessment for all levels and areas of the education system

The nature of post-conflict reconstruction means that there is often a lot of damage caused to schools and colleges and disruption of education programmes, with little data on needs, and sometimes insecurity and inaccessibility. Lack of roads, hotels or other accommodation, and insecurity made it difficult to conduct needs assessment in eastern counties of Liberia, for example, when plans for reconstruction were being prepared in the mid-1990s.

The most pressing concerns are likely to be school materials, school shelter and the payment of teachers. In the short-term, external agencies may be willing to help with materials, temporary shelter and even reconstruction of schools. However, no-one wants to make a long-term commitment to pay normal teacher salaries, which constitutes a major part of the education budget. Occasionally, a donor is willing to pay salaries for a short period of time, but this can be less than helpful if it creates expectations that the government cannot subsequently meet from its own revenue. It is better to look for sustainable policies or approximations such as *Food for Work* incentives to teachers from the *World Food Programme*. This may mean starting with new under-educated and untrained teachers and training them on the job. However, training is more fundable than recurrent costs from the viewpoint of donors.

Strategies to supplement school resources or attract teachers receiving low salaries:

		Advantages	Disadvantages
School fees		• Typically part of the pre-conflict culture • Some children can attend school • Difficult to implement good schemes for exemption of disadvantaged children	• Some children might not be able to attend school • Fees might not meet resource needs or provide adequate supplementary income to teachers
School or teacher agriculture or income generation support (cash crop, animal husbandry, bees)		• Sustainable (but often ineffectual since school administration, parents and teachers may not be good managers of income-generating activities) • Typically part of the pre-conflict culture • Educational opportunity in regard to teaching agriculture, business, and animal husbandry	• Students, often of one gender, are often used for labour in the school fields, taking away from them time during which they could be studying. • Takes school administrators' time away from education
Teacher housing incentives	**Houses on school compound**	• Can enhance school's permanent capital	• May hinder permanent settlement of families since they are living on school property • Creates a precedent
	Houses off school compound	• Can enhance school's permanent capital	• Creates a precedent
Food for work		• Helps meet teachers' basic needs	• Cannot continue indefinitely

Paying school teachers for additional work on externally-sponsored supplementary education projects, such as adult literacy or youth work	• Provides services for other portions of the population • Lays the groundwork for future national programmes	• Potentially overworks teachers and school administrators • Potentially unsustainable by the community and by the government
Creation of a mentoring system for teachers in which mentoring teachers receive an incentive	• Increases the quality of education • New teachers get training on the job which may lead to (better) paid employment later	• May be unsustainable • Financially assists mentors only

Source: Adapted from Triplehorn (2002).

Mobilizing external resources

As noted previously, some crisis situations receive high publicity and are overwhelmed with initial approaches from donors and NGOs, while for others the reverse is true. In any case, if external resources are needed, it is important for the government to appoint a donor relations manager with a good grasp of both qualitative and quantitative aspects of education, and international experience.

It is true that donors' attention is often focused on certain regions of the world where they have particular interests. But the principal donor countries have embassies in most countries; and staff in these embassies wants to be active! Hence, there is a good chance of donor funding for an activity that donors consider important and which has a high likelihood of succeeding. Poor funding often reflects donors' doubts about the effectiveness of implementation of suggested projects.

Hence, it is important for the government to identify good education projects, to explain them using concepts (such as gender equity, quality improvement) that donors consider important in order to show evidence of implementation capacity, and to establish good personal relations with donor officers handling the education sector.

In some cases, there is a *United Nations Consolidated Appeal* to cover initial reconstruction costs. These appeals may follow a calendar year or, occasionally, other timeframes related to the timing of a crisis. (These appeals also cover emergency situations such as disasters, refugee movements, etc.) UN agencies, and sometimes NGOs, submit project proposals with a time-horizon of about 12 months. The government should review these proposals before they are finalized. The primary purpose of the *Consolidated Appeal* is to improve communication between international agencies, and for donors to see that duplication of requests is avoided. The Appeal does not necessarily generate funds, which normally have to be requested directly from donors themselves. If the government has good relations with donor representatives, it can advocate with them for funding of proposals, which it considers important.

The short-term focus of the *Consolidated Appeal* mechanism, which was set up to deal with humanitarian emergencies, means that other approaches to donors are needed to provide the longer term support necessary for the reconstruction of education. The *World Bank* may be able to assist and/or advise on approaching other donors such as regional development banks. The *European Union* is an important donor, despite being reputed for having slow bureaucratic procedures. Bilateral assistance is often more flexible and can be used to get special programmes off the ground quickly.

Donors want to see sustainability in the programmes they support, so that their departure will not lead to the collapse of the programmes they supported. On the one hand, this means that low cost programme models should be adopted, since they have a greater chance of sustainability. On the other hand, the appeals to donors should stress that sustainability will take a considerable amount of time since, for example, communities cannot contribute substantial resources to education programmes until the process of reconstruction has restored their livelihoods. Interim steps, such as training communities in procedures for school management and development, can be included in the proposals put to donors. It is also important to reflect the contribution of local communities in the documentation submitted to donors, for example their contribution of time and physical labour to the construction of classrooms, volunteer inputs to pre-school classes and activities for youth, and so on.

Co-ordination of national and international actors

In most reconstruction situations there are assistance agencies or local NGOs and often donors involved. The government must take the lead and provide strong leadership to co-ordinate the NGOs and donors offering assistance in order to ensure a coherent programme. If necessary, the government should ask for education specialists to be deputed to the Ministry to help with co-ordination and to build up expertise of national counterparts.

There is often a policy of allocating particular locations to particular assistance agencies. Care should be taken to identify relevant mandate limitations, and negotiate ways of coping with these. For example, agencies focusing on children will normally have limited interest in education at secondary and post-secondary levels and in non-formal or vocational training (except possibly for women). They should be asked to take responsibility for these activities or arrange for a partner agency to do so. Likewise, agencies with a refugee focus must work with partners who can continue to support reconstruction after the limited period during which they can work with returnee communities and link them in advance with appropriate sources of funding.

Development of transitional and medium-term policies and plans for educational reconstruction

As soon as possible, work should begin on both a short-term and a medium-term policy framework and plan. It has been suggested that there is an 18 to 24 month post-crisis period, during which ideas for an improved education system can take hold before people and institutions become rigid in their approach (Vargas-Baron and McClure, 1998). Decisions taken (or not taken) early on, for example regarding teacher payments or building specifications, can create problems later on.

The actual structure of a plan can vary according to local circumstances and preference. The structure may not look very different from that of a normal plan, but the content will reflect the impact of the conflict or disaster. The *National Education Master Plan* for Sierra Leone (1997-2006), prepared with wide stakeholder participation, reads in a conventional way even though the education system was severely damaged. The six major objectives of the plan are to:

- increase access to basic education;
- develop a broad-based education system;
- improve the quality and relevance of education;
- expand and upgrade technical/vocational education;
- promote adult literacy, non-formal and informal education;
- develop relevant attitudes, skills and values in children.

In a well-received five-year plan developed by the Palestinian National Authority in 1999, the first chapter presented the educational context: historical background, the status of education in 1994 when the Authority inherited an education system 'nearing collapse', a description of the education system, the schools, the accomplishments achieved between 1994 and 1999 and the perspective for the future. The second chapter presented the challenges facing the Authority and its development plan, the education policy framework, the specific objectives for the five-year education plan and their financial implications.

Objectives of the Five-Year Education Development Plan of the Palestinian National Authority: 2000/2001 – 2004/2005

"General objectives …to bring about the reform and improvement of the Palestinian education system and enable it to meet new requirements emerging at the dawn of the 21st century:

1. Provide access to education for all children.
2. Improve the quality of education.
3. Develop formal and non-formal education.
4. Develop the management system for planning, administration and finance.
5. Develop the human resources of the education system.."

Each general objective is supported by three to nine 'specific objectives' and by specific 'targets' for implementation.

Source: Palestine, Ministry of Education (1999: 36).

The particular headings for general objectives in this plan could have been different. For example, staff training could have been included under each of objectives 2 to 4, but because of its importance, 'human resource development' was treated as a separate objective, not least because donors see this as an investment that will have a long-term benefit.

Although the plan may have a conventional outline, the content will reflect the crisis which the country has suffered. The principles outlined in *Chapters IV to VII* above can serve as a checklist for plan preparation.

X. Applying these principles: perspectives of other actors

NGOs

There is not one international NGO that has pre-eminence in the field of emergency education, although several do produce excellent work. Hundreds of national and local NGOs also work on emergency education, often with support from their international counterparts and the United Nations. Education is needed in every neighbourhood affected by crisis, and many NGOs therefore get involved worldwide. There is a substantial problem in establishing communications with all these NGOs to review best practice and reflect together on the principles that can be derived from them. The overview presented in this booklet represents a personal view of what is, or should be, common ground. A formal inter-agency process to develop shared standards for emergency education is being initiated under the aegis of the *Inter-Agency Network for Education in Emergencies* (see *Chapter XI*).

Policy development

Each NGO likes to develop its individual identity and its own policy framework. By participating in international fora, these policies can be, to some extent, harmonized at the level of principles while somewhat differentiated according to the philosophy of the implementing agency. As mentioned earlier, however, there can be difficulties when NGOs or their donors interpret their mandates narrowly and have a restricted vision of emergency education; for example, when a child-focused NGO supports primary education, but does not adequately address the need for secondary education in the locations where it is in action through supporting such education or nominating partners to do so.

More generally, NGOs that are cut off from the mainstream of policy debate often see education in terms of its narrowest interpretation, such as *'chalk and talk'* only with no outreach to the wider community. NGOs need to face the implications of their interest in schooling in situations of emergency and post-crisis recovery. The principles developed above suggest that: NGOs should not take on the narrow task of providing classrooms, blackboards and teachers if they are not prepared also to take on the wider task of providing access to education enriched with recreational (among other) activities and messages needed especially by emergency-affected children and young people. The NGOs or their partners should also meet the needs for education and related activities for out-of-school children and young people, and also for adults. Otherwise, donors may think that they are funding 'education' for a crisis-affected population, when in reality all that they are supporting is a narrow concept of schooling for those children who are fortunate enough to be able to attend school.

The policy framework will address many other issues. An international NGO should have a policy for capacity-building of its local staff (and, where applicable, government officers), child protection, inclusiveness and gender, willingness to work with displaced populations after their return home, and other issues referred to in this booklet.

Preparedness

Emergencies are unpredictable and often vary greatly from one to the next. It is inevitable that a policy framework will reflect recent experience and provide a less-than-perfect fit to the needs of future emergencies.

Nevertheless, NGOs can take certain steps to permit rapid and effective response. These include:

- a clear policy on rapid response and emergency education in general;
- arrangements for deployment of staff at short notice;
- seed money that permits local expenditures at short notice, rather than awaiting approval of a new project by donors;
- authorization to purchase core education materials in advance of the needs assessment, based on population totals;

- training all the NGOs' field education staff in the basics of emergency education, so that they can respond quickly to an emergency in the country where they are employed or on deployment elsewhere;
- including elements of emergency education in the training of senior managers and programme staff in the organization, so that the case does not have to be drafted from scratch in the heat of an emergency;
- planning for sustainability – planning early for handing over the long-term management of programmes to local institutions.

Insisting on standards

NGOs often implement emergency education programmes with funds raised from donors such as UN agencies or bilateral agencies. They often negotiate with programme or budget officers, who have little knowledge of education issues. The NGOs are in a strong position because the donor wants to fund education for a crisis-affected population and the NGO is willing and able to deploy staff there. It is the NGO's responsibility to tell donors that it is futile to provide education without also providing a substantial proportion of in-service teacher training; that community workers are needed to motivate and guide the setting up of *School Management Committees*; that recreational activities with associated non-formal and informal education for out-of-school youth are life-saving and vital to the future of the community; that the community needs and wants peace education; and so on. These standards should be insisted upon before the NGO signs the contract.

Moreover, the NGO needs to specify the locally appropriate resourcing standards that are required, including class size, supply of textbooks, teacher incentives, shelter standards, for example cement floors and rain-proof roofs (in rainy climates), and materials that can be shared between schools if necessary, such as sports equipment, library books and simple science equipment. There should be a clear and mutually recognized plan to move towards the specified standards within a period of 18 months to three years, according to the circumstances. If the donors fail to provide the resources to meet the agreed standards, and offer only regrets and excuses that carry little hope of remedy causing restricted access to education and lower standards, then the NGO can take the matter up at higher levels in the *world of government* and with NGO *rights watch advocates*. Often the key people within donor agencies do not realize the impact on the education of crisis-affected populations caused by budget cuts that are intended to achieve other objectives, such as reducing bureaucracy in the *United Nations* (UN), or phased reduction of geopolitical commitments to a particular region.

It is true that there are weak emergency and reconstruction education programmes worldwide at the present time. This is no reason, however, for an NGO that is associated with an emergency education programme to let that programme fall below a reasonable and agreed standard of resourcing and effectiveness. NGOs should see their role as including the transmission of information from the field to the donor agencies, including both the intermediary donors, such as UN agencies, and actual donor governments.

UN agencies

Various UN agencies are involved in education in crisis and reconstruction. Key actors are UNHCR and UNICEF, the former having a lead role in supporting education for refugees, and the latter in supporting education for other populations. As noted earlier, UNICEF focuses especially on early childhood and primary schooling, but may also support secondary education, education for out-of-school adolescents and for women, according to local circumstances. Both these agencies are able to raise substantial funds for working with crisis-affected populations thanks to donors' contributions. Some of this funding is earmarked to specific sectors including education; in addition, some un-earmarked funds can be allocated according to the agency's assessment of need, and this may favour education.

UNESCO has a mandate to cover all aspects of education but tends to work 'upstream' on policy and system building, particularly with government ministries of education, finance and planning. UNESCO has to seek funding earmarked for activities within its mandate of *education, science* and *culture*, rather than the broader range of life-saving activities covered by UNICEF and UNHCR. It is, nevertheless, trying to build donor confidence so that it may increase its level of 'extra-budgetary funding'. Specialist units of UNESCO are making 'niche' contributions to education in emergencies and reconstruction, according to their skills and mandates. For example, the International Bureau of Education (IBE/UNESCO) has developed expertise in advising governments and agencies on curriculum change and social cohesion in conflict-affected societies. Likewise, the International Institute for Educational Planning (IIEP/UNESCO) is engaged in developing resources to train government ministries and other agencies in the planning and management of education in conflict, emergency and reconstruction.

The *World Food Programme* plays a major role in emergency education through providing food for school meals and food-for-work for activities such as teaching, attending teacher training sessions, construction of schools, participation in adult education and training sessions etc. Other programmes include the use of food (or empty food containers) as an incentive, as in the highly successful programme for Afghan refugee girls and female teachers in Pakistan, who receive a tin of edible oil for each month of regular attendance in their refugee schools.

Other UN agencies are involved in emergency education from time to time in connection with school construction, school health programmes, gender issues and so on.

Policy development

UNHCR issues guidelines on refugee education policy (UNHCR, 1995). At the time of writing, revised guidelines are under internal discussion. Much remains to be done to disseminate this policy to UNHCR staff, some of whom are more positive about education than others. Since about half of all refugees are children and young people, it is important that UNHCR's approach to refugee protection and assistance towards a durable solution includes a clear policy for refugee education.

UNICEF has stressed that its policy for education in emergencies is to lay the foundation from Day One for rebuilding education in a way that provides a sound basis for future educational development (Pigozzi, 1999).

It will be useful if the UN agencies further develop their policies and guidelines for support to educational reconstruction. They should use their moral authority to argue against educational structures and policies that may promote divisions in society in the future, such as the idea of providing separate curricula for the different ethnic groups in post-war Bosnia in the 1990s. The UN agencies should bring such issues to the forefront of the international political dialogue.

Preparedness

UNICEF has developed a 'core corporate commitment' to respond to emergencies within a few days. This can lead to expensive initiatives such as bulk transportation of educational materials by air (especially as UNICEF's rules make speedy local procurement difficult).

UNHCR, likewise, has emergency teams ready to respond within hours, but these teams do not, at the time of writing, include education experts. Education response is included in the responsibilities of the emergency team's *Community Services Officer.* The attitude of many staff towards education in early emergency has often been ambiguous or negative, in contrast to the concerns of refugees who prioritize education. The situation has been improved in recent years, with the deployment to UNHCR field operations of standby refugee education co-ordinators from a roster maintained by the *Norwegian Refugee Council.*

UNESCO works with government ministries of education to enhance their preparedness for emergencies. The agency plans to contribute to preparedness by developing training courses and modules for education in emergency and reconstruction, notably through the International Institute for Educational Planning.

Insisting on standards

UN agencies play an important role in monitoring and reporting on the adequacy of emergency education programmes and sensitizing donors to resourcing deficits. Normally there is a tendency to report positively on achievements, but this may be contrary to the interests of those persons the agencies are supposed to protect. Are donors, or the politically conscious public in donor countries, aware of the poor conditions of schools for refugees or internally displaced populations in conflict-affected areas? Are they aware that literacy programmes for refugee women in several countries are severely constrained by lack of modest amounts of funding, or have been discontinued due to budget cuts?

UN agencies should insist that NGOs receiving their funding meet the principles of best practice described in this booklet and work in a co-ordinated fashion to implement them.

Donors

Donors have shown increasing interest in education for conflict-affected populations. However, some donors have separate sections concerned with 'humanitarian' and 'development' assistance, and do not include education in the former category. The problem originates in the kind of semantic problem described in the opening chapter of this booklet. 'Humanitarian', like 'emergency', is a term that in general speech refers to a sudden dangerous crisis which threatens life and health. In the context of disasters and conflict, however, a complex humanitarian emergency may last for years or even decades. Education cannot be delayed until the climate moves from a sense of 'humanitarian' crisis to 'development assistance'.

It is more fruitful to consider that crisis-affected children and adolescents are the adults of the near future and that investment in their education is both:

(a) a response to their immediate and personal needs; *and*
(b) an investment in development and peace.

Education for crisis-affected populations should thus be funded from both humanitarian and development budgets.

Recent pronouncements by donor governments suggest a growing acknowledgement that humanitarian response to emergencies includes education. This was made explicit at the Winnipeg *Conference on War-Affected Children* in September 2000, at which all participants, including the major donor governments, issued a declaration which included the statements that, *"Education must be a priority in humanitarian assistance ... Education is central to humanitarian action."* (Winnipeg *Conference on War-Affected Children*, 2000). The Governments of Norway and Canada have described education as the 'fourth pillar' of humanitarian response, along with food/water, health and shelter (Johnson, 2002: 4; Government of Canada, 2000). The Government of Sweden has explicitly affirmed the importance of a thorough educational response during emergencies (Appadu, 2002).

Policy development

It is difficult to discern the policies of donor governments towards education in situations of crisis and emergency. In fact, policy documents and web sites describing national assistance policies towards developing countries sometimes provide little detail concerning support to education beyond a commitment to supporting basic education for all. Some donors do indeed provide consistent funding for refugee education, specific emergencies and reconstruction programmes, but the issue needs to be brought more forcefully into the domain of public policy. It is an issue that will not simply go away, but will become all the more important as education levels rise and crisis-affected children need support for more years of schooling.

Preparedness

The Norwegian Government has set a particularly good example with its fast-track procedure for committing funds for emergency education response, notably funding secondment of education co-ordinators to UNHCR or UNICEF field operations within a matter of hours or days rather than weeks or months.

In contrast, one NGO education manager remarked to the author that *its major bilateral donor required a well-developed project proposal based on a field appraisal, and time to process this according to normal channels.* Subsequently, the proposal for emergency psychosocially-oriented quick response is approved too late, thus any funds sent arrives at the field when formal schooling has already been resumed.

Insisting on standards

Some donors keep a watchful eye on emergency education programmes by involving their embassies in field visits and monitoring activities. In general, however, there is a lack of concern about the adequacy of these programmes. The Executive Committee of UNHCR, for example, which includes both donor countries and countries hosting refugees, does not systematically ask for comprehensive feedback on refugee education, despite awareness that about half of the caseload consists of children and young people eligible for education and training. Feedback on the education of internally displaced populations or those affected by crisis and instability is often minimal.

Donors should spell out for themselves the principles and standards applicable to their support for emergency-related education in general and for specific individual programmes that they fund. This is the first step towards accountability and effective use of resources.

Donors should further insist on monitoring and evaluation based on these principles. They should require reporting not only of inputs and enrolments, but also of *gaps*: gaps in access, gaps in safe and healthy classroom provision, gaps in programmes for out-of-school young people, gaps in teacher training, and gaps in peace education, as well as positive achievements. This will permit donors to consider reallocation of additional resources to meet their standards and principles.

XI. Reflections and concluding remarks

We conclude with a consideration of *how education can help prevent conflicts and disasters* and by taking a *look at the future development in the field of education in emergencies.*

Can education help prevent conflict?

There is now an increasing awareness that education can be a divisive factor in society, in some instances leading to violent conflict (Tawil, 1997; Bush and Saltarelli, 2000), or a factor which contributes to social cohesion and peace-building. Smith and Vaux (2002) have reviewed the overall relationship between education and conflict, while Isaacs (2002) has presented a matrix of 'conflict indicators' which can be used for early warning purposes. Both came to the conclusion that inequities and inadequacies within the education system can push young people towards conflict.

When we look at these writers' implicit or explicit recommendations on education policies that lessen the risk of conflict, we find that one of the best ways for educators to prevent conflict is to address issues of educational access, resources, activities/curricula and governance/co-ordination. Thus, it seems that the consensus principles of the emergency education movement outlined in *Chapters IV* to *VII* above are not luxuries, but necessities to prevent conflict or a recurrence of conflict.

Simplifying the presentations of Smith and Vaux, and Isaacs, one can show the resemblance as below.

123

Issue	Conflict prevention issues/ early warning indicators (Smith and Vaux, 2002; Isaacs, 2002)	Emergency Education Principles (*Chapters IV–VII* above)
Access	Is there a systematic bias in access of different groups to education? Are minority groups treated inclusively and with respect? Do all children have access to schools in their vicinities and languages? Are girls attending school in equal numbers to boys from primary to post-secondary?	Is there access to education, recreation and related activities for all levels of education, with gender sensitivity and inclusive of all groups? Does education serve as a tool of protection? (*Chapter IV*)
Resources	Is there an intentional or unintentional bias in inputs? Is there equitable recruitment of male and female teachers from different ethnic groups with a sufficient number of teachers fluent in the students' mother tongues? Are costs affordable by middle and low-income families? Is there committed support to teachers, through salaries and training? What percentage of the budget is allocated for education?	Do education programmes draw on the human resources of the affected communities, providing training for those serving as teachers? Do teachers receive incentives at least sufficient to meet the opportunity costs of their work? Are resourcing standards clearly defined and adequate to meet the educational and psychosocial objectives? (*Chapter V*)
Activities and curriculum	Are there recreational activities for young people? Do school religious education policies or language aggravate tension? Do the textbooks for history, geography and cultural subjects tell a 'national story' that casts certain national groups or neighbouring countries as bad and the dominant group as good? Is there an active programme that focuses on building skills, values and knowledge supportive of a peaceful future? Are there gender biases or stereotypes in teaching materials? What percentage of educational resources goes to	Do young people have access to education, recreation and related activities, helping meet their psychosocial and developmental needs? Do curricula support long-term national development (with language policies for refugees supporting their future repatriation and reintegration) and are they enriched with life skills for health, safety, environmental awareness, peace/conflict resolution, tolerance, human rights and citizenship? (*Chapter VI*)

	teacher training, curriculum and textbook development and research? Do nation-building reforms support equity, inclusion, diversity, reconciliation and tolerance?	
Governance and co-ordination	Is there transparency, accountability and inclusiveness of all stakeholders in education decision-making? Does decentralized decision-making support this or strengthen ethnic divisions and exclude women? Do plans and education reform packages incorporate a conflict analysis of the education sector? Are there clear policy positions to remedy divisive elements such as ethnicity, gender inequality, religion, and poverty? Who are the stakeholders and are they represented in public policy consultations, national and regional committees?	Is there community involvement in the management of schools? Are there co-ordination mechanisms bringing together all stakeholders in the emergency education response? Is there capacity building to provide for transparent, accountable and inclusive system management by local actors? (*Chapters IV* and *VII*)

Prevention of new emergencies thus implies that governments and agencies that support emergencies should follow principles similar to those of emergency response, including adequate resourcing for education. This should be reflected in *Education for All Strategy Papers, Poverty Reduction Strategy Papers*, and development planning generally. The alternative to investing in education and education reform may be destruction of the education infrastructure and disruption of the national economy through civil conflict.

Education in emergencies: the future

Is education in emergencies a coherent subject or a sub-discipline? Will it be part of the curriculum in the future, in universities and in training programmes for education professionals? What will be the future development of this subject? What are the possibilities for international co-operation in this area? These and other questions could be discussed at length but will be tackled briefly here. 125

■ *Is education in emergencies a coherent sub-discipline of education?*

Emergency education in many ways resembles education in non-emergency situations, but has its own distinctive features. It can be seen as a sub-discipline in its own right, or as a module within sub-disciplines such as education for development, comparative international education, and educational planning and management.

The special features of education for populations affected by conflict, calamities and instability may be grouped as the context and the core.

- The *context* is the range of crisis and post-crisis scenarios and their implications for organizing, resourcing and co-ordinating access to education and related activities.
- The *core* is the special features of the education and other structured activities, presented here as the principles of healing, curriculum policy oriented to long-term solutions for displaced persons and to national curriculum renewal and curriculum enrichment with life skills for health, safety, conflict resolution and citizenship.

Much of the international discourse on education in emergencies relates to large-scale conflicts or disasters. Some of the discourse is relevant, likewise, to smaller crises such as local floods, earthquakes, other disasters or local conflicts, which also entail contextual logistical and resourcing issues and the substantive need for trauma healing for students and teachers and relevant life skills. This links education in emergencies to the worldwide movement for national and local disaster-preparedness.

There is some overlap with education in 'silent' crises such as the HIV/AIDS epidemic, economic downturns/structural reforms, or education for street children or other underprivileged groups. These crises have their own contextual framework, but many overlap in terms of the core needs for psychosocial and life skills education.

There is some overlap, likewise, with personal and interpersonal issues that trouble schools and teachers in all countries and situations. In many countries there are large numbers of students affected by conflict or sickness in the home, family break-up or bereavement; and there is widespread bullying or sexual exploitation in schools. Elements of education in emergency relate to these situations, notably in respect of meeting psychosocial needs of conflict-affected or bereaved students, and training in life skills such as assertiveness and conflict prevention.

The table below shows the relationship between education in large-scale emergencies (the discourse in this booklet) and other situations.

'Education in major emergencies' seen in relation to other crises

	Major conflict or disaster	Local crises	'Silent' emergencies	Interpersonal, classroom & playground conflicts
Context				
Scenarios for access, resources and co-ordination	Large-scale actions	Small-scale actions	Varied scales of action	School-level action
Core				
Psychosocial response / trauma healing	definitely needed	definitely needed	definitely needed	definitely needed
Curriculum framework	definitely needed	may be needed	may be needed	may be needed
Life skills for health, safety, environment	definitely needed	definitely needed	definitely needed	definitely needed
Life skills for conflict prevention, citizenship	definitely needed	definitely needed	definitely needed	definitely needed

■ *Will emergency education be part of the curriculum in the future, in university courses and practitioner training programmes?*

Education as a response to crisis situations is relevant to courses in crisis management and humanitarian relief (within the field of international relations and regional studies). Within the discipline of education as such, the ground covered in this text is especially relevant to courses in education for development, comparative international education and educational planning and management.

A large proportion of *developing countries* have suffered war, instability and major disasters in the last quarter of the twentieth century, and almost all are at risk of natural disasters, at least. Christopher Talbot, staff member of the International Institute for Educational Planning (IIEP/UNESCO), suggests that "*the study of education for development should include response to intermittent crises of varying types and magnitudes*". In today's world it is not realistic to draw up plans where all variables progress smoothly towards a better future, without also having preparedness for setbacks and unforeseen problems.

Within a university course on education for development or comparative international education, one would therefore expect to see a module on education in emergencies. In training programmes for government officials on educational planning and management, there should likewise be a module on education in emergencies, with an emphasis on the implications for national policy.

Within teacher-training programmes, it may be useful to combine studies of education for populations affected by conflict and natural disasters with studies relating to 'silent emergencies' prevalent in the country concerned. By preparing and encouraging teachers to deal with the crises in their neighbourhood and school, they may be more able to respond if there is a large-scale catastrophe. Faculty members and teacher trainers can develop their knowledge of emergency education by working intensively with teachers during local emergencies, and can subsequently share their experience and research findings with the wider international community.

■ *Building a database through and for research*

Research into emergency education is difficult because emergency response is rarely well documented. The emphasis of governments and NGOs is on dealing with the crisis on a day-to-day basis, and documentation is weak. Reports are scattered irretrievably as 'grey literature' among the files of the numerous organizations working in this field. Personal recollection is often unsatisfactory as a source of information, all the more so because in the early stages of an emergency, staff are often deployed, or consultants hired, on a short-term basis of a few weeks or months. In the longer term, there is often a high rate of staff turnover due to difficult conditions. Within governments, there is often a transfer of staff from one job to another.

What is needed is a culture of real-time documentation and research. At the time of writing, a number of organizations are beginning case studies to improve the documented knowledge base for emergency education. However, in this field situations evolve rapidly and information is often out of date before it is published. The donors supporting case studies should incorporate funding for a watching brief to follow up and record the evolution of each situation over a period of at least five years. This is less time than is needed to reconstruct a destroyed education system and to reach consensus on contentious issues of curriculum.

Most organizations at field level prepare quarterly and annual reports for their headquarters. An inter-agency agreement on making these and other reports publicly available would be most valuable (sensitive elements could be excluded). Governments could assist this process by requiring agencies to publish a full annual report of education activities undertaken in their countries.

■ *What are the next steps?*

The reader is invited to develop his or her own ideas regarding the development of the field of education in emergencies. Some possible aspirations are shown in the table below.

Some aspirations for education in emergencies

Access	Donors require, and/or agencies send them, full reports from each field operation on current access to and inclusiveness of education
	Agencies adopt and publish policies that prioritize 'schooling' (including secondary education) rather than only primary education, and promote access to tertiary education including through open and distance learning
Resources	Agencies prepare and make public clear target resourcing standards for each emergency education programme
	Agencies adopt specific emergency education policies and have seed money for immediate action in future crises
	Universities in donor and crisis-affected countries offer Masters' courses, including education in emergencies, thereby upgrading the quality of staffing of field programmes
Activities and curriculum	Agencies and concerned governments accept an integrated life skills programme as standard practice for schooling and non-formal education, including skills for conflict prevention, citizenship, health, gender equity and environmental conservation
	Agencies and concerned governments adopt a framework for curriculum auditing that excludes conflict-generating and gender-biased elements and incorporates model peace-building and gender-equitable behaviours (also health and environmental messages)
Co-ordination and governance	Measures to promote social cohesion and acceptance of diversity included in national and Education for All education plans and in project proposals
	Strong inter-agency co-operation at global and national levels for adoption of good practice approaches, and active network of researchers

■   *What are the priority areas for co-operation among practitioners?*

There have been various attempts to create an international network of concerned NGOs and UN agencies. The *Refugee Education Consultation* held in 1990 as a follow-up to the Jomtien Forum on *Education for All* was intended to lead to ongoing co-operation, but the impetus was quickly lost. Another attempt was made in connection with the mid-decade review of progress in 1996. An important web site supporting information sharing on emergency education was established at that time: the *Global Information Networks In Education* (www.ginie.org).

One difficulty in networking has been that many organizations have only one technical staff member at headquarter level to handle education or emergency education, and this person is overloaded with operational and bureaucratic tasks. Moreover, when these staff members resign or are rotated to other posts, their personal investment of time and effort in the network is lost, and the next incumbents may not feel committed to the network role that they have inherited. Another factor has been the practical difficulty of communicating with field staff, and the cost of face-to-face meetings. It is hoped that in the era of e-mails and conference calls, some of these constraints may be overcome.

The Dakar Conference on *Education for All* was followed by a meeting in Geneva in November 2000, hosted by UNHCR, jointly with UNESCO, UNICEF and leading NGOs, which led to the creation of the *Inter-Agency Network for Education in Emergencies* (INEE). INEE has benefited from the services of a full-time co-ordinator funded by the *Mellon Foundation* and the NGO CARE. The role of the network is primarily for information exchange, advocacy, and the development of shared guidelines and materials. INEE is facilitating a consultative process designed to lead to 'standards' and guidelines for emergency education, similar to those prepared for humanitarian response in other sectors (Sphere Project, 2000). INEE may also give its endorsement to materials prepared by members, and has already endorsed generic materials for peace education in emergencies and reconstruction (INEE, 2002). INEE keeps members up-to-date through its list-serve and has a website containing suggestions for good practice. It is hoped that INEE will continue its work while there is a need, and readers are cordially invited to become members. See also www.ineesite.org for details.

References

Aguilar, P.; Retamal, G. 1998. *Rapid educational response in complex emergencies: a discussion document.* Hamburg; Paris: UNESCO/IIEP (www.ginie.org).

Appadu, K. 2002. *Education in situations of emergency, conflict and post conflict.* Stockholm: Swedish International Development Co-operation Agency.

Arnhold, N.; Bekker, J.; Kersh, N.; McLeish, E.; Phillips, D. 1998. *Education for reconstruction: the regeneration of educational capacity following national upheaval.* Wallingford, Oxfordshire: Symposium Books.

Asian Development Bank; World Bank; UNDP. 2001. *Preliminary needs assessment for Afghanistan* (draft). Manila: Asian Development Bank.

Avery, A.; Bobillier, C.; Sinclair, M. 1996. *Source book for refugee skill training.* Geneva: UNHCR.

Baxter, P.; Fisher, J.; Retamal, G. 1997. *Mine awareness education.* Geneva: UNESCO/International Bureau of Education.

Baxter, P. 2000. *UNHCR Peace Education Programme.* Geneva: UNHCR.

Baxter, P. 2001. "The UNHCR peace education programme: skills for life." In: *Forced Migration Review*, vol. 11, pp. 28-30 (www.fmreview.org).

Bird, L. 1999. *The Tanzanian experience.* Dar es Salaam: UNICEF (www.ginie.org).

Brown, T. 2001. "Improving quality and attainment in refugee schools: the case of the Bhutanese refugees in Nepal." In: Crisp, J.;

Talbot, C.; Cipollone, D. (Eds.) 2001, *Learning for a future: refugee education in developing countries,* pp. 109-161. Geneva: UNHCR; see also www.unhcr.ch.

Burde, D. 1999. *Communities, conflicts and pre-schools: an evaluation of Save the Children's Early Childhood Education Programme in Croatia and Bosnia-Herzegovina.* Westport: Save the Children Federation/USA.

Bush, K. D.; Saltarelli, D. 2000. *The two faces of education in ethnic conflict: towards a peacebuilding education for children.* Florence: Innocenti Research Centre, UNICEF (www.unicef.org).

Canada (Government of). *Background Paper to Winnipeg Conference on War Affected Children.* 10-17 September 2000, Winnipeg.

Dall, F. 2001. *Building local capacity for literacy services in Guatemala.* Washington D.C: *Save the Children Federation/USA.*

DANIDA. 1996. *The international response to conflict and genocide: lessons from the Rwanda experience.* Copenhagen: DANIDA (www.um.dk/danida).

Dykstra, A. 2002. "Education in crisis: development sequence and transitions." In: Miller, V.W.; Affolter, F.W. 2002, *Helping children outgrow war.* Washington D.C: USAID.

Englbrecht, W. 2001. "Bosnia and Herzegovina – no future without reconciliation." In: *Forced Migration Review*, vol.11, pp. 18-21 (www.fmreview.org).

Fountain, S. 1997. *Education for conflict resolution: a training for trainers manual.* New York: UNICEF.

Fountain, S. 1999. *Peace education in UNICEF.* New York: UNICEF (www.unicef.org).

Gillespie, A. 2002. *Skills-based health education to prevent HIV/ AIDS: the case against integration.* New York: UNICEF (www.unicef.org/programme/lifeskills/priorities/placement.html and www.unicef.org/programme/lifeskills/sitemap.html).

Inter-Agency Network for Education in Emergencies (INEE). 2002. *Peace Education Programme.* Geneva: UNHCR.

International Federation of Red Cross and Red Crescent Societies (IFRC). 2002. *World Disasters Report.* Geneva (www.ifrc.org).

International Save the Children Alliance (ISCA). 1996. *Promoting psychosocial well-being among children affected by armed conflict and displacement: principles and approaches.* Geneva: ISCA.

Isaacs, A. 2002. *Education, conflict and peacebuilding: a diagnostic tool.* Ottawa: CIDA.

Johannessen, E. 2000. *Evaluation of human rights education in southern Caucasus.* Oslo: Norwegian Refugee Council.

Lange, E. 1998. *The IRC education programme for refugees in Guinea, 1991-1998: a best practice study.* Geneva: UNHCR.

Lowicki, J. 2000. *Untapped potential: adolescents affected by armed conflict.* New York: Women's Commission for Refugee Women and Children.

Lyby, E. 2001. "Vocational training for refugees: a case study from Tanzania." In: Crisp, J.; Talbot, C.; Cipollone, D. (Eds.) 2001. *Learning for a future: refugee education in developing countries,* pp. 217-259. Geneva: UNHCR.

Machel, G. 1996. *The impact of armed conflict on children.* New York: United Nations (www.unicef.org).

Machel, G. 2001. *The impact of war on children: a review of progress since the 1996 UN report on the Impact of Armed Conflict on Children.* London: Hurst.

Macksoud, M. 1993. *Helping children cope with the stresses of war: a manual for parents and teachers.* New York: UNICEF.

McCallin, M.; Jareg, E. 1996. "The rehabilitation and social reintegration of child soldiers." In McCallin, M. (Ed.) *The psychosocial well-being of refugee children: research, practice and policy issues*, pp. 192-217. Geneva: International Catholic Child Bureau.

Midttun, E. 1998. *Brief history and main features of the TEP for Angola 1995-8, as developed and extended by the Norwegian Refugee Council, by arrangement with UNESCO-PEER.* Oslo: Norwegian Refugee Council.

Midttun, E. 2000. *Education in emergencies and transition phases: still a right and more of a need.* Oslo: Norwegian Refugee Council.

Miller, V.W.; Affolter, F.W. 2002. *Helping children outgrow war.* Washington D.C: United States Agency for International Development.

Nicolai, S. 2000. *Emergency education in East Timor: lessons learned.* New York: International Rescue Committee.

Nuttall, J. 1999. *Bosnia pre-school programme: some lessons learned about design and management.* Westport: Save the Children Federation/USA.

Obura, A. 2002. *UNHCR Peace Education Programme: evaluation report.* Geneva: UNHCR.

Palestine, Ministry of Education (1999). *Five-year education development plan 2000-2005.* Ramallah: Ministry of Education.

Pigozzi, M. 1999. *Education in emergencies and for reconstruction: a developmental approach.* New York: UNICEF (www.unicef.org).

Retamal, G.; Devadoss, M. 1998. "Education in a nation with chronic crisis: the case of Somalia." In: Retamal, G; Aedo-Richmond, R. (Eds.) 1998. *Education as a humanitarian response*, pp. 74-93. London: Cassell.

Retamal, G.; Aedo-Richmond, R. (Eds.) 1998. *Education as a humanitarian response.* London: Cassell.

Rhodes, R; Walker, D.; Martor, N. 1998. *Where do our girls go?: Female dropout in the IRC-Guinea primary schools.* New York: IRC.

Rugh, A. 2001. *Models, policy options, and strategies: a discussion paper in support of Afghan education.* New York: UNICEF.

Sinclair, M. 1988 *Evaluation of UNHCR vocational training programmes in Baluchistan Province, Pakistan.* Unpublished.

Sinclair, M. 2001. "Education in emergencies." In: Crisp, J.; Talbot, C.; Cipollone, D. (Eds.) 2001. *Learning for a future: refugee education in developing countries*, pp. 1-83. Geneva: UNHCR (www.unhcr.ch).

Sommers, M. 1999. *Emergency education for children.* Cambridge: Mellon Foundation/MIT.

Sommers, M. 2001. "Peace education and refugee youth." In: Crisp, J.; Talbot, C.; Cipollone, D. (Eds.) 2001. *Learning for a future: refugee education in developing countries*, pp. 163-216. Geneva: UNHCR (www.unhcr.ch).

Sommers, M. 2002. *Children, education and war: reaching Education for All (EFA) objectives in countries affected by conflict.* Washington, DC: Conflict Prevention and Reconstruction Unit, World Bank (www.worldbank.org).

Sphere Project. 2000. *Humanitarian charter and minimum standards in humanitarian response.* Geneva: The Sphere Project of the Steering Committee for Humanitarian Response (www.sphereproject.org).

Swedish Save the Children. 1999. *Mines beware! Starting to teach children safe behaviour.* Stockholm: Rädda Barnen/ Save the Children Sweden

Smith, A.; Vaux, T. 2002. *Education, conflict and international development.* London: Department for International Development.

Talbot, C.; Muigai, K. 1998. "Environmental education for refugees: guidelines, implementation and lessons learned." In: Retamal, G; Aedo-Richmond, R. (Eds.), *Education as a humanitarian response*, pp. 223-247. London: Cassell.

Tawil, S. (Ed.) 1997. *Final report on case studies of the workshop on educational destruction and reconstruction in disrupted societies.* Geneva: UNESCO/IBE.

Tawil, S. 2000. "International humanitarian law and basic education." In: *International Review of the Red Cross*, no. 82, pp. 581-600.

Tefferi, H. 1999. *Psychosocial needs of children in armed conflict and displacement.* Stockholm: Rädda Barnen/Save the Children Sweden.

Tolfree, D. 1996. *Restoring playfulness: different approaches to assisting children who are psychologically affected by war or displacement.* Stockholm: Rädda Barnen/Save the Children Sweden.

Triplehorn, C. 2002. *Guidance notes for education in emergencies* (www.ineesite.org).

UNESCO. 1999. *The right to education: an emergency strategy.* Paris: UNESCO.

UNHCR. 1995. *Revised guidelines for educational assistance to refugees.* Geneva: UNHCR.

UNHCR. 1997a. *Evaluation of UNHCR's efforts on behalf of children and adolescents.* Geneva: UNHCR (www.unhcr.ch).

UNHCR. 1997b. *Review of UNHCR's education activities.* Geneva: UNHCR (www.unhcr.ch).

UNHCR. 1999. *Tanzania Refugee Programme Community Services and Education Report.* Geneva/Dar es Salaam: UNHCR.

UNHCR; Save the Children Alliance. 2000. *Action for the Rights of the Child: training modules.* Geneva: UNHCR; Rädda Barnen/ Save the Children Sweden.

UNHCR. 2002a. *Refugees and others of concern to UNHCR: 2001 statistical overview.* Geneva: UNHCR (www.unhcr.ch).

UNHCR 2002b. *Peacemaker: the peace education newsletter, issue no. 4.* Nairobi: UNHCR.

UNICEF (n.d.). *International guidelines for landmine and unexploded ordnance awareness education.* New York: UNICEF (www.unicef.org).

UNICEF. 1998. *Let's become familiar with natural disasters.* Skopje: UNICEF.

UNICEF. 1999. *Honduras report: lessons learned after the impact of Hurricane Mitch in the education sector.* Geneva: UNICEF.

UNICEF. 2001. *Technical notes: special considerations for programming in unstable situations.* New York: UNICEF.

UNOPS. 2002. *Rehabilitation and social sustainability operational guide: education.* Geneva: UNOPS.

Vargas-Baron, E.; McClure, M. 1998. "The new heroics of generational commitment: education in nations with chronic crises." In: Retamal, G; Aedo-Richmond, R. (Eds.), *Education as a humanitarian response*, pp. 271-288. London: Cassell.

Wilkinson, R. 2000. "We will forgive...we will never forget." In: *Refugees*, vol. 1, no. 118, pp. 4-15.

Winnipeg Conference on War-Affected Children, 2000. *Caught in the crossfire no more: a framework for commitment to war-affected children.* 2000. Final statement (http://www.waraffectedchildren.gc.ca/crossfire-e.asp).

World Education Forum. 2000a. *Education for All 2000 assessment: Framework for Action.* Paris: International Consultative Forum on Education for All, UNESCO (www.unesco.org).

World Education Forum. 2000b. *Thematic study: education in situations of emergency and crisis.* Paris: International Consultative Forum on Education for All, UNESCO (www.unesco.org).

WHO; UNESCO. 1994. *School health education to prevent AIDS and STD: a resource package for curriculum planners.* Geneva: World Health Organization and UNESCO; re-issued by UNAIDS, Geneva.

IIEP publications and documents

More than 1,200 titles on all aspects of educational planning have been published by the International Institute for Educational Planning. A comprehensive catalogue is available in the following subject categories:

Educational planning and global issues
General studies – global/developmental issues

Administration and management of education
Decentralization – participation – distance education – school mapping – teachers

Economics of education
Costs and financing – employment – international co-operation

Quality of education
Evaluation – innovation – supervision

Different levels of formal education
Primary to higher education

Alternative strategies for education
Lifelong education – non-formal education – disadvantaged groups – gender education

Copies of the Catalogue may be obtained on request from:
IIEP, Dissemination of Publications
information@iiep.unesco.org
Titles of new publications and abstracts may be consulted at the
following web site: *http://www.unesco.org/iiep*

The International Institute for Educational Planning

The International Institute for Educational Planning (IIEP) is an international centre for advanced training and research in the field of educational planning. It was established by UNESCO in 1963 and is financed by UNESCO and by voluntary contributions from Member States. In recent years the following Member States have provided voluntary contributions to the Institute: Denmark, Finland, Germany, Iceland, India, Ireland, Norway, Sweden and Switzerland.

The Institute's aim is to contribute to the development of education throughout the world, by expanding both knowledge and the supply of competent professionals in the field of educational planning. In this endeavour the Institute co-operates with interested training and research organizations in Member States. The Governing Board of the IIEP, which approves the Institute's programme and budget, consists of a maximum of eight elected members and four members designated by the United Nations Organization and certain of its specialized agencies and institutes.

Inquiries about the Institute should be addressed to:
The Office of the Director, International Institute for Educational Planning,
7-9 rue Eugène-Delacroix, 75116 Paris, France.